GOOD POLICING

Trust, Legitimacy and Authority

Mike Hough

With a foreword by
Tom Tyler

T0339398

P

First published in Great Britain in 2021 by

Policy Press, an imprint of
Bristol University Press
University of Bristol
1–9 Old Park Hill
Bristol
BS2 8BB
UK
t: +44 (0)117 954 5940
e: bup-info@bristol.ac.uk

Details of international sales and distribution partners are available at
policy.bristoluniversitypress.co.uk

British Library Cataloguing in Publication Data
A catalogue record for this book is available from the British Library

ISBN 978-1-4473-5507-6 paperback
ISBN 978-1-4473-5509-0 ePub
ISBN 978-1-4473-5508-3 ePdf

Cover design: by blu inc, Bristol
Front cover image: Alamy/D. Hale Sutton

Bristol University Press and Policy Press use environmentally
responsible print partners.

Printed and bound in Great Britain by CMP, Poole

Contents

List of figures, tables and boxes

Figures

Tables

Boxes

About the author

Mike Hough is Emeritus Professor at the School of Law, Birkbeck, University of London. Prior to his academic career, he was a researcher in the Home Office, where he was one of the small team that designed the British Crime Survey (now Crime Survey for England and Wales). He left the Home Office as Deputy Director of Research in 1994 to set up a research centre at London South Bank University. He and his centre relocated to King's College London in 2003 as the Institute of Criminal Policy Research (ICPR). In 2010, he and his team moved to Birkbeck, University of London. From 2004 until his retirement in 2016, he was University of London Professor of Criminal Policy. ICPR is one of the major UK centres for academic policy research on criminal justice. Mike's research interests include: procedural justice theory; public perceptions of crime and punishment; crime measurement and crime trends; and sentencing. He has around 300 publications. He was President of the British Society of Criminology from 2008 to 2011 and the European Society of Criminology awarded him the 2020 ESC European Criminology Award in recognition of his lifetime contribution to European criminology.

Acknowledgements

Most of the research that I have conducted on the police over the last two decades has been collaborative, and this book synthesises the findings of many of these projects. I owe a huge debt of gratitude to a wide range of colleagues in England and elsewhere. These include Ben Bradford, Andrew Coyle, Diego Farren, Vicki Herrington, Jonathan Jackson, Jessica Jacobson, Stefano Maffei, Tiggey May, Juan Carlos Oyanedel, Paul Quinton, Julian Roberts, Sebastian Roché, Mai Sato, Betsy Stanko and many others. I should also apologise in advance for instances in this book where I have oversimplified or misrepresented our collaborative work. I am particularly grateful for comments on earlier drafts from Ben Bradford, Diego Farren, Jessica Jacobson, Gemma Lousley, Mai Sato and Thomas Tapmeier. I would also like to thank Rebecca Tomlinson and the editorial team at Policy Press for their patience and all their help.

I should acknowledge the many insights I have got into policing in the course of working with staff in police forces and with related bodies, including the College of Policing, Her Majesty's Inspectorate of Constabulary, Fire and Rescue Services, the Independent Police Complaints Authority and the National Audit Office. I have spared individuals the embarrassment of being identified but I hope they know who they are.

Our work in this field has been generously supported by many funders, and this book draws on research findings funded by several bodies, notably, the European Commission (Eurojustis, Grant no. 217311, and Fiducia, Grant no.290653), and the UK Economic, Social and Research Council (Grant Numbers RES-178-25-0008, ES/LO11611/1 and ES/L016656/1).

Foreword

Tom Tyler

Macklin Fleming Professor of Law and
Professor of Psychology
Yale University

Unlike the UK, the US has never had a discussion about what good policing should be about. Rather, US policing has moved forward as a series of improvised solutions to immediate problems of social order. This began with informally organised community watch patrols, and has included the police in the South acting as slave patrols, while police forces in northern cities have served the interests of ward bosses in industrialising cities. These efforts have primarily addressed the needs of prevailing local power and have not reflected a discussion among all of the members of particular communities about what democratic policing should be about. In the US, this style of policing by improvisation has fitted well within a long tradition of local political control of the police and the courts.

During the 1970–80s, US police defined themselves largely in terms of addressing ongoing crime waves. During this era, the police focused their organisations around combating violent, often drug-related, crime. They defined their mission as harm reduction through crime management. This definition of the police largely, or solely, in terms of fighting crime continues to this day. The predominance of harm reduction via crime control as the goal of US policing has combined with a force-based model of legal authority. Police officers have been trained and deployed to use force to compel compliance.

This conception of policing would seem to leave little room for concerns about popular legitimacy in discussions of policing. However, during the 20th century, the US has paid a heavy price for failing to seriously engage with the need to address issues of police–community relations. One part of that heavy price is through the recurrence of outbreaks of urban unrest like the riots that occur periodically within US cities. The pattern of police misconduct, followed by protests, riots and destruction, continues. Equally troubling is that these events happen within a general climate of public distrust and, often, open hostility between the police and the communities that they patrol and, at least in theory, protect. Police use of force fuels distrust and anger. Distrust and anger promotes crime, undermines cooperation and, periodically, provokes collective violence. In this context, it is telling that over the last 30 years, while crime rates in the US have plummeted, trust in the police in American communities has not risen. Studies consistently show that approximately 40 per cent of Americans distrust their local police, and percentages are considerably higher among the members of minority groups.

There have been some efforts to address the popular legitimacy of the police in the 20th century. The first major national effort occurred in the mid-20th century following widespread urban protests in the 1960s, when the Kerner Commission (1968) examined the causes of that disorder. That commission advocated a more direct role for the police in helping to address social problems within communities. The argument for a more cooperative police–community relationship led to the idea of community policing as a model designed to bolster the popular legitimacy of the police. However, this innovation was rapidly overshadowed by the police efforts to address crime in the 1970s and 1980s mentioned earlier, and popular legitimacy became a peripheral police concern.

A National Academy of Sciences report issued in 2004 (Skogan and Frydl, 2004) pointed to the success of police efforts to manage crime but called for a refocus on the issue of police–community relations, in particular, the popular legitimacy of the police. Attention to the importance of popular legitimacy has steadily increased since that time, so much so that the Task Force on 21st Century Policing (President's Task Force, 2015) suggested that building community trust in the police must be the first task of police forces (the first pillar of policing). In the 21st century, good policing has increasingly come to mean policing that leads to popular legitimacy within policed communities.

As popular legitimacy has emerged as a more central issue in US policing, a key concern has been with understanding how the police might create and sustain their legitimacy. As this volume makes clear, how people who hold power can transform their power into legitimacy so that it will be accepted among the general public is hardly a new question. European sociologists (Emile Durkheim and Max Weber) and psychologists (Freud) were all preoccupied with identifying ways in which modern societies could promote the appropriateness of their authority and encourage the public to accept and defer to the modern state. This issue is very much alive today in relationship to US policing, as well as in the UK.

Procedural justice theories have been a key development for policing because they provide a proven way to build legitimacy. These theories originated in US social psychology and began to emerge as a coherent set of ideas for policing in the 1970s as they were demonstrated in field research to influence public behaviours like obeying the law. We live in an instrumental age, and authorities might be forgiven for thinking that people react to their interactions with them in terms of the outcomes they provide (Did the police apprehend the person who robbed me? Did the police solve the problem I called them about?). The central insight behind procedural justice is that people do not evaluate legal or political authorities primarily in terms of the outcomes they receive from them. Rather, people evaluate these authorities as being legitimate if they judge them as exercising their authority fairly.

In particular, people evaluate the police and courts against their standards for fair procedures for exercising legal authority. Those standards include: whether they were given a chance to state their case; whether they were given explanations for decisions; whether those decisions were neutral and fact-based; whether respect was shown for their rights as citizens and for them as people; and whether they inferred that the authorities were sincerely trying to do what was good for the people they were dealing with.

My own work on procedural justice dates from the early 1980s and has become more important as these issues have assumed a more central place in discussions about what democratic policing should involve. Procedural justice puts the focus on what the people in the community think is appropriate, which is a core feature of democratic discussions.

The history of policing is different in England. Early on, Sir Robert Peel, when founding the London police in 1829, pointed to the centrality of community trust to policing. This tradition has continued, aided by a stronger national-level police force, as well as by the generally lower levels of lethal force that generally prevails in British society. The police do not routinely carry guns, nor do citizens or most criminals. These differences notwithstanding, as this volume makes clear, legitimacy is still a central concern of policing in the UK, as well as more broadly in Europe.

Given these differences in policing, I find it particularly gratifying to see the take-up of procedural justice ideas in Europe, and in the UK in particular, over the last two decades. The theoretical and empirical contributions of scholars such as Tony Bottoms and Justice Tankebe in Cambridge, and Jonathan Jackson, Ben Bradford and Mike Hough in London, have been significant. I first met Mike at a Russell-Sage Foundation-sponsored conference in Paris in 2004; thereafter, I was involved with the European Union (EU)-funded Eurojustis project led by Mike and his colleagues. This led to their large-scale comparative test of procedural justice theory, using the European Social Survey, which is discussed in this volume. This was a major piece of work, showing that the key relationships between trust, legitimacy, compliance and cooperation posited by the theory could be found in 26 European countries. This European-wide project has been the key evidence that has moved discussions about procedural justice from an American idea to a model of global policing.

My own background is as a researcher, and I believe that the research case for procedural justice-based models of policing is strong. However, whatever the research evidence may say, getting police departments to adopt principles of procedural justice has not always been easy. The occupational culture of front-line officers in many countries does not sit very comfortably with principles of procedural justice, nor does the management style of 'old-style' police leaders in some departments. Many politicians are also reluctant to advocate an approach that is nuanced and lacking a hard edge and populist appeal. This is especially true in the US, where politicians have regarded being viewed as 'soft on crime' as the beginning of the end of their careers. It is important to convey the key messages of procedural justice theory to these audiences in an accessible way. This book does this well. It is tailored to meet the needs of non-academic audiences in the UK but should also have broader appeal. As the data presented make clear, this approach is not just applicable to the US and the UK; it is supported throughout Europe. While it is beyond the scope of this volume, recent studies, in fact, suggest that it may well be supported throughout much of the world.

As I noted, the failure to resolve fundamental conflicts between the police and American communities has led to recurrent cycles of conflict. I am writing this in the aftermath of the killing of George Floyd by a police officer in Minneapolis. His death is unfortunately only the most recent in a succession of killings by US police officers of black men. Readers in the UK and elsewhere might reasonably ask what they have to learn from a body of thought developed in a country where such tragedies continue to occur. There is no question but that the unhappy history of black slavery and the past and ongoing issues of injustice in the treatment of indigenous people and the members of different immigrant groups form a challenging background for US policing because it has created a climate of distrust in the police and courts in many communities. This is exacerbated by a frontier heritage that has led to high levels of private gun ownership, an emphasis on the local control of law enforcement, a punitive popular culture that glorifies 'get tough' solutions to problem like crime and a long tradition of anti-intellectualism, as reflected in distrust in expertise and evidence-informed policy making. The US is a challenging policing environment. That being said, the US is not alone in facing many of the these types of problems, and I hope that other countries can benefit by learning from the solutions that my country is still so painfully struggling to put into place. A good beginning for those who would like to do so is to read the clear and complete discussion of these ideas contained in this volume.

1

Introduction

This book sets out an argument about the nature of crime control and the implications for good policing. It draws on criminological research, in particular, on procedural justice theory, but it is not intended as an academic work. It aims to synthesise the work of an international network of police researchers who have developed ideas of trust in the police, police legitimacy and compliance with the law. This introductory chapter first provides some context for a discussion of good policing. It then summarises my arguments in brief – in a way that I hope will provide the reader with a clear sense of the book's direction of travel. I am a British academic and crime and its control in Britain are my main points of reference; however, the book's conclusions have, I hope, wider applicability.

Crime control and its regulation: the policy context

Crime is as old as the social institutions that have evolved to regulate it. In the distant past when humans began to make the transition from hunter-gathering to farming and lived in small agrarian groups, there was conflict, for certain, but no crime – as there were no formal systems of justice. The last two millennia have seen the evolution of increasingly institutionalised systems for regulating conflict. Ancient cultures had well-developed systems of law, and in Europe, elements of Roman law formed the foundation of law from the Middle Ages onwards.

Many of us have a mindset that leads us to believe that in most areas of life, 'things are getting worse', and it is certainly true that most people have a pessimistic view about law and order, thinking that crime and disorder are on the rise. However, any cool-headed assessment of long-run trends in crime, especially in violent crime, would conclude the opposite. This countervailing and more optimistic position has been most clearly articulated by the 20th-century sociologist Norbert Elias, and more recently popularised by the North American academic Steven Pinker.[1] They – and I – would argue that the long-run trend from mediaeval times can be characterised by greater self-restraint, less violence and more respect for the rights of others. Certainly, the best historical analyses of trends in violence are consistent with this perspective.[2]

No one would want to deny that there have been oscillations around this downward trend. The move from agrarian to urban societies in the 18th and 19th centuries probably triggered spikes in various forms of crime – and in concern about crime. Two world wars and the Holocaust also evidence the capacity for state violence on a grotesque scale. There was also a rapid growth of crime of all sorts in the second half of the 20th century in most industrialised countries – followed by an equally rapid fall, which in the UK began in the mid-1990s.

The politics of law and order are shaped by the way in which our attention is grabbed by these oscillations around the downward trend, rather than by the long-run pattern. Spikes in crime get much more attention than falls. Our personal security and protection against crime is of great importance to us, and we are sensitised to any threat to our security. Consistent with the insights of Kahneman and Tversky's 'prospect theory',[3] we are much more sensitive to losses – whether these are losses in money or in safety – than we are to gains. Thus, the rise in violence in UK cities since around 2012 has been a source of great – and understandable – concern, even if violent crime has not reached the levels seen two decades earlier. The gains in safety went largely unnoticed – and undiscussed outside of criminology – but the reversal of the trend for some types of high-harm violent crime (in particular, knife crime) has attracted a great deal of attention.[4]

Public anxiety about worsening crime creates great pressure on politicians to produce credible responses – and given that the solutions that they offer are seen by most people through the refracting lenses of the popular press, solutions deemed credible are usually simple ones. At the time of writing, Prime Minister Boris Johnson was promising 10,000 more prison places, greater police stop-and-search powers and longer prison sentences: 'We need to come down hard on crime. That means coming down hard on criminals. ... I want the criminals to be afraid – not the public' (Johnson, 2019).

The elements of this simple version of deterrence theory[5] are as follows: the world is divided into the law-abiding and criminals; we all respond rationally to deterrent threat, though some need heavier threats than others; and if criminals fail to respond to current deterrent threats, the weight of punishment simply needs to be increased. In reality the research evidence to support simple deterrence theories of this sort is thin. Certainly, some people who break the law are rational calculators, and when the probability of punishment is high, most of us are fairly responsive to threat. However, in situations where there is less certainty of punishment, deterrent effects are hard to isolate. There are many reasons for this. Many of us behave impulsively and spontaneously, without thinking through the consequences. We often act under pressure or encouragement from others. Our judgement may be impaired by alcohol or illicit drugs. The threat of punishment can also prompt defiance, rather than compliance. Furthermore, punishment inevitably dispossesses people of things that they value – money, possessions or freedom – and sustained and heavy punishment eventually confers on the punished the freedom of the dispossessed. (People have greater freedom – of a sort – the less that they have to lose.) This is not to argue that order can *never* be maintained by holding the population in a deterrent 'grip of steel'; however, it is only one choice out of several that are open to politicians and criminal justice leaders, and one that can bring heavy and needless costs. The choice architecture facing politicians is such that they are driven to advocate deterrent strategies – because they believe that these are vote-winners. In particular, they tend to opt for increasing the severity of punishment rather than its certainty or celerity because this can be readily achieved through legislation.[6]

Yet, there is an alternative narrative about the regulation of crime, which has had currency since the establishment of the Metropolitan Police in 1829. This is that people consent to the rule of law, and that this consent can be consolidated or withdrawn depending on the way that the police and justice systems operate. This perspective recognises that criminal justice is a formal system of control that sits alongside the less formal mechanisms for reproducing order that are embedded in parenting, religious and educational institutions, and the workplace. These systems of informal control are probably more significant than formal justice systems in shaping levels of crime in most cultures and in most settings. They establish norms of behaviour to which most people subscribe most of the time. Formal criminal justice can be thought of as a backup system that supplements these informal mechanisms.

If deterrence theories place the police and the courts at the centre of crime control, accounts that stress normative compliance – where people obey the law because they feel that it is *right* to do so – imply that other factors play a much larger role. The dynamics of political debate make it hard for politicians to acknowledge this publicly. Those in government will want to demonstrate to their electorate that they are taking firm and decisive action to tackle crime problems, and their political opponents will do their best to show that government policies are weak and ineffective. Within this logic, politicians can rarely create sufficient space in public debate to recognise that the levers of government are only quite loosely linked to crime problems, which are in large part the products of the interplay between cultural and socio-economic factors and the shifting opportunities for crime.

Nevertheless, there are periods when political reliance on principles of rational deterrence gives way to a recognition that public consent to the rule of law can be fragile, and that if damaged, it is important to shore up public trust in the justice system. For example, the late 1970s and early 1980s saw serious challenges to police legitimacy in Britain, first of all with the emergence of corruption scandals within the Metropolitan Police, then followed by a series of urban riots – some of which were inescapably about the over-policing of minority ethnic groups. This prompted a range of political responses stressing the need to shore up the legitimacy of the police. At the time, I was a researcher in the Home Office, and I can attest to the lively and intelligent debate among ministers, their senior civil servants and the Metropolitan Police Commissioner about the right balance to be struck between securing 'the Queen's peace' and law enforcement.[7] However, by the 1990s, a markedly more populist climate had emerged, together with a managerialist approach to police management, where 'crime-fighting' targets became the norm. Since then, in their public pronouncements, both the main political parties have adhered to the simple deterrent narrative of crime control– however subtle and perceptive their private conceptions of policing might have been.

The book's argument in a nutshell

Much criminological research aims to explain *why people break the law*. While this is certainly a reasonable ambition, it draws attention away from an equally important but much-ignored question: *why do most of us obey most laws most of the time?* Sensible answers to this question inevitably make reference to the norms and standards that we generally live by. This book offers an extended critique of the idea of people as rational calculators who respond to deterrent threats issued by the state by weighing up the personal costs and benefits of complying with – or defying – the criminal law. Certainly, in much of our lives, we often behave as the *homo economicus*[8] of classical economic theory, choosing courses of action that maximise utility. However, when it comes to moral, legal and quasi-legal rules, it is far from clear that we act in this way.

These rules are established by individuals, organisations or institutions that claim *authority* to do so, and whose claims to be rule-makers are accepted by those who are rule-takers. When people accept that rule-makers are entitled to create (and sustain) systems of rules and to command obedience to these rules, they are conferring *legitimacy* on the authority of the rule-makers – they are accepting that those in authority have a *right* of some sort to demand compliance with their rules. This analysis applies whether we are talking about authority wielded by parents, teachers, religious figures, bosses in the workplace or, of course, officers of the law.

The processes by which people come to confer authority on others, and choose to comply with their instructions and rules, have little to do with rational calculation about personal costs and benefits. It is well beyond the scope of this book to describe in any detail how parents, teachers, religious figures or managers establish their authority – except to say that the processes by which it is established are complex psychological ones, usually involving attachment, identification and a sense of belonging. There are also – potentially more troubling – sources of authority, such as charismatic power, which is easy to recognise but hard to analyse.

This book is less concerned with the mechanisms that energise these informal systems of social control and is more concerned to identify what legitimates the authority of state institutions such as the police, in particular, how the police can build and consolidate – or squander – their legitimacy. It pays considerable attention to the sorts of factor that may legitimate the authority of the formal institutions of justice, such as the police and the courts. I shall argue that police authority is built by engendering different forms of public trust: trust that the police will be fair and respectful in their treatment of the policed; trust that they will not discriminate in favour or against different groups; trust that their decision-making arrives at fair outcomes; and trust that they achieve an acceptable level of competence. The book's central thesis is that: first, if the police secure public trust, people will regard their authority as legitimate; and, second, if people confer legitimacy on the police, they will comply with the law and police demands, and cooperate with the police. Styles of policing that privilege the building of police legitimacy in the eyes of the public should operate in support of, and in harmony with, less formal systems of social control.

The arguments in the book draw extensively on procedural justice theory – or, as it is sometimes called, the 'procedural justice model'. The three central claims of procedural justice theory are that:

- in people's contact with police and other justice officials, procedural fairness – especially the quality of treatment that they receive – is more important to them in the course of contacts with justice officials than securing an outcome that is to their advantage;
- trust in the fairness of the police, especially in their procedural fairness, leads people to confer legitimacy on the police; and
- when people confer legitimacy on the police, this results in both compliance with the law and cooperation with justice officials.

An important claim made by procedural justice theory is that securing compliance with the law by deploying normative strategies such as those derived from procedural justice theory is less costly, less intrusive and more effective than instrumental or coercive ones based on deterrence. I do not want to argue that tough, deterrent policing is necessarily and universally ineffective. However, I suggest that maintaining a convincing level of deterrent threat has high financial and social costs, and that securing consent to the rule of law can achieve more stable and more peaceful communities. Equally important, the more that 'hard' policing tactics are deployed, the less room the police leave themselves for policing by consent. Hard policing can result in *hard power traps* – an issue to which we shall return in Chapter Two.

Procedural justice and theories of policing

What sort of theory is procedural justice theory? And how does it fit into the landscape of policing theories? The sociology of the police now has a 60-year history in developed industrialised countries, and this body of work has been concerned with four main aspects of policing: 'What is the mandate of modern policing institutions?'; 'What do they actually do?'; 'What functions or outcomes flow from these activities?'; and 'What are the mechanisms or processes by which the outcomes are achieved?'

This is not the place to offer a summary of this body of work,[9] but a few points need to be made in order to enable me to locate work on procedural justice within it. Common-sense thinking about policing would tell us that the police mandate is to reduce crime. The sociologist Egon Bittner's work remains very widely cited as providing an important redefinition of this mandate; his two most quoted passages[10] are probably his characterisation of police work as 'something-that-ought-not-to-be-happening-and-about-which-somone-had-better-do-something-now!', and his statement of the unique competence of the police:

> The specific capacity of the police is wholly defined in their capacity for decisive action. ... More specifically, that the feature of decisiveness derives from the authority to overpower opposition in the 'then and there' of the situation of action. *The policeman, and the policeman alone, is equipped, entitled, and required to deal with every exigency in which force may have to be used to meet it.* (Emphasis in original)

Bittner's account of the police as an *emergency* service whose effective delivery relies on the capacity of deploying coercive force was – and remains – consistent with accounts of what the police in developed countries actually do. An extensive body of descriptive work has shown that crime fighting takes up a minority of police time; the common thread to incidents dealt with by the police is that their resolution may involve the deployment of force. The potential need to deploy coercive force is, of course, very different from the actual use of force; it is a truism that effective police work avoids the use of coercive force wherever possible.

On the functions served by the police, it is widely accepted in the UK that the police exist to 'preserve the Queen's peace' but this can clearly mean different things to different people. Is this the peace that serves the best interests of the 'ruling classes', the wealthy or the general population? This book will not address this question head-on, though it resurfaces in Chapter Six. The point I want to make here is that institutions such as the law and the police can serve different interests, and can do so in different ways. Procedural justice theory offers one sort of explanation of the processes by which those in authority secure compliance from the population and the acceptance of a given form of social order. First and foremost, procedural justice theory offers a descriptive account of the ways in which power-holders can transform their power into authority, enabling them to secure compliance without resorting to coercive force. It is a social-psychological theory about legitimacy and the ways in which that legitimacy shapes the interactions of individuals – and individuals' relationships with organisations – which is not in itself prescriptive. Certainly, the theory carries practical implications but it is not usually presented as value-laden. However, submerged in most procedural justice scholars' accounts (including my own and those of my colleagues) is a more political concept of legitimacy that is highly prescriptive.[11] We advocate procedural justice styles of policing partly on their practical merits but also because of a sense that they embody the *right* way in which people in authority should relate to those over whom they can exercise power.

In this respect, procedural justice theory overlaps with ideas about 'responsive regulation', in particular, associated with John and Valerie Braithwaite.[12] The central idea in responsive regulation is that regulatory strategies – in policing or any other form of regulation – can be arranged in a pyramid. The least intrusive modes of regulation – encouragement and persuasion – are at the base of the pyramid, with increasingly more intrusive strategies as one moves up the pyramid, from warnings and statements of intent, to sanction, to light punishment and then to heavy punishment and incapacitative strategies. The key claim in responsive regulation is that in pursuing compliance, the regulatory authority should always select the least intrusive strategy that will secure compliance. The guiding principles are that regulation should be used as sparingly as possible, and that it should be applied with respect and fairness. Advocates of responsive regulation have rendered explicit the normative foundation of their ideas to a greater degree than procedural justice theorists but the two approaches have a great deal in common.

The shape of this book

The rest of the book will proceed as follows. Chapter Two will set out in more detail the concepts that underpin the idea of 'good policing' that I am arguing for. It will consider what is meant by legitimacy and legitimate authority, and will discuss the sorts of factors that are likely to build or corrode police legitimacy. It will argue that different forms of trust can be sources of police legitimacy but that trust in the police is not a synonym for police legitimacy. However, this is not the whole story as the police form part of the state; therefore, the legitimacy of political institutions and the social justice that these manage – or fail – to achieve will inevitably tone the way in which the public views the police. It will consider the dynamics that can lead policing into hard power traps, and how to avoid them. It concludes by sketching the beginnings of a definition of good policing. Chapter Three will summarise the empirical research that underpins the procedural justice perspective. It will argue that there is good evidence for the core argument that trust in the police serves to legitimate police authority, and that police legitimacy serves to secure compliance with the law and cooperation with the police. This chapter will offer some social-psychological explanations for the importance that people attach to receiving fair and respectful treatment from the police. Chapter Four examines the policing of minority groups, in particular, minority ethnic groups, considering how similar – but not identical – patterns of discrimination and distrust can be traced in many industrialised countries. Chapter Five discusses the preconditions needed for embedding principles of procedural justice in police organisations. It argues that if police leaders want their workforce to treat the public with fairness, dignity and respect, the same values must permeate police management. It also identifies the role of, and limits to, training and education. Chapter Six explores some of the ethical dilemmas and risks associated with the style of policing advocated in the book. In particular, there is a risk that front-line police will regard values of fairness, decency and respect simply as shortcuts for securing compliance, and will simply 'role play' a display of these values. There is also a possibility that procedural justice in policing may provide an 'ideological cloak' for masking broader social inequity. It offers what I hope is a persuasive resolution to these ethical issues. Chapter Seven offers some final thoughts about the links between law, ethics and morality, on how the police can support public norms and values, and on how, at the same time, the police should ensure that their remit is firmly grounded in the law, rather than moral norms.

This book was finished as the coronavirus pandemic reached its peak, and the Postscript offers some reflections on policing when emergency legislation introduces tight restrictions on freedom of movement. Policing the pandemic strained both political and police legitimacy, and the reasons are worth exploring.

2

Trust and legitimacy: the basic ideas

> Law enforcement agencies should adopt procedural justice as the guiding principle for internal and external policies and practices to guide their interactions with rank and file officers and with the citizens they serve. (President's Task Force, 2015: 1)[1]

Authority is the legitimate right of one person or group to exercise power over another. The sociologist Max Weber identified three main types of authority: *traditional, charismatic* and *rational-legal*. The clearest examples of authority derived from tradition can be found in hereditary monarchies and the authority that religious leaders such as the Pope can command by virtue of tradition and rituals of appointment. *Charismatic* authority exists where an individual leader has extreme and rare powers of attraction. The impact of charisma can be benign or malign, and it clearly carries political risks, as exemplified by the rise of right-wing populist political leaders since the turn of this century. *Rational-legal* authority is derived from coherent systems of rules and regulations, whose value can be demonstrated or at least argued for.

Politicians, political scientists and commentators are all centrally preoccupied by the processes by which political power is legitimated and therefore sustained. They take for granted that power relations achieve stability only if naked power is transformed into authority by processes of legitimation. Surprisingly, given that the police are that arm of the state that has a near-monopoly on the use of coercive force against citizens, legitimacy has not been a concept that has pervaded political and academic debate about policing. Rather, it has emerged, become submerged and re-emerged as reputational threats to the police have come and gone. In Britain, systematic police corruption in the 1970s and the urban riots of the 1980s threw issues of police legitimacy into sharp focus. Throughout the Troubles in Northern Ireland, the legitimacy of the now-disbanded Royal Ulster Constabulary was a perennial source of concern there.[2]

However, for much of the last 30 years, mainstream politicians in mainland Britain have largely ignored issues of legitimacy, and focused on tough, no-nonsense solutions to crime. The start of this period of 'penal populism'[3] can be dated to 1992/93, when Tony Blair, as Labour shadow Home Secretary, announced that he would be 'tough on crime, tough on the causes of crime', which earned the response from the Conservative Home Secretary Michael Howard that 'prison works'.

Rhetoric of this sort can be seen in penal politics from then until the present day.[4] Thus, on becoming Home Secretary in 2010, Theresa May told the police that 'Your job is nothing more, and nothing less, than to cut crime.'[5] This statement may have been good politics at the time but it was sociologically illiterate. In similar vein, ten years later, Home Secretary Priti Patel told police leaders that in exchange for more resources, they *must* cut crime: 'In three years' time, when the 20,000 additional officers are through the door, the people will want to see a difference. Less crime. Safer streets. No excuses. The public won't accept excuses, and neither should we.'[6]

It cannot be said that either police leaders or academic commentators have ignored issues of legitimacy. It is true that, in the last century, this was not a central preoccupation in either policing circles or academia – with some important exceptions.[7] However, since the turn of the century, legitimacy studies and procedural justice theory have become central to police studies, and key policing institutions have adopted this perspective.[8]

Defining legitimacy

Power is legitimate, and thus transformed into authority, when its use follows rules that are regarded as fair by both the power-holders and those over whom power is exercised, and when the latter confer their consent to the use of this power. The value of Weber's insights to the Machiavellian politician is, of course, that compliance derived from authority is more stable, and much less painfully bought, than that which is tightly linked to the deployment of coercive force. When spelt out in this way, few would take issue with these basic principles; however, as many writers have observed, legitimacy is a difficult and slippery concept.

The reason for this is that the term is used in two main ways, which have important differences. First, political philosophers and political commentators use the term to characterise the quality of political regimes. They might argue that a particular dictatorship lacks legitimacy because it fails to meet a series of fairly well-agreed 'rule of law' criteria, such as: democratically elected politicians; political honesty; judicial independence; judicial adherence to principles of legality; robust processes of appeal; and policing systems that are impartial, honest and fair, and observe due process. This use of the term is usually called 'normative' or 'objective' legitimacy: 'normative' because it makes reference to a set of recognised norms or standards; and 'objective' because factual evidence can be found to support or reject a claim that a state (or its institutions) is failing to meet these standards.

'Legitimacy' is also used to refer to the subjective assessment that people make of an authority to which they are subject. When people accept the legitimacy of an authority (a government or one of its institutions, or a politician or a law officer), this means that, in their view, the authority is entitled to command their compliance, and that they feel a duty, or moral obligation, to comply with what the authority requires of them. This use of the term is usually referred to as 'empirical' or 'subjective' legitimacy: 'empirical' because it refers to individual and measurable assessments of authority made by those who are subject to that authority; and 'subjective' because the research is establishing perceptions of legitimacy, rather than any external reality.[9]

Clearly, there is a good deal of overlap between an authority's legitimacy as seen by a group of political scientists and its legitimacy as seen through the eyes of those who are subject to that authority. However, there may be important divergences. First, an authority can fail significantly to meet the criteria of legitimacy agreed by political scientists while still commanding support from large sectors of the governed. The early period of Hitler's Germany is one example. Trump's presidency might count as another for those who think that truthfulness was an early victim of his tenancy of office, and abuse of electoral due process another; however, his 'base' appears to have had no concerns on such scores. Specifically in relation to police legitimacy, people in some countries may support extra-legal tactics such as the 'crossfire' shooting of known criminals,[10] crackdowns on political demonstrators and – more mundanely – 'cutting corners' to get results.[11] In other words, people may want police to 'play by the rules' but the rules that they support may not always align strictly with legality.

Second, an authority can meet all the generally agreed set of criteria of legitimacy while failing to command any sense of moral obligation or obedience among those who are subject to that authority. Examples come less readily to hand but it is easy to conceive of an objectively legitimate authority whose standing in the eyes of the public is successfully undermined, for example, by hostile media coverage and effective attacks from political opponents. Alternatively, authorities can be trapped by history, for example, where police try unsuccessfully to rebuild trust and recover their legitimacy among communities that have experienced coercive styles of policing for many years.

These mismatches between normative and empirical legitimacy account for some of the disagreements about the definitions of legitimacy in academic research. The criteria for normative legitimacy are quite narrow, and relatively uncontentious, relating to the achievement of ethical standards in politics – or, in our case, policing. The criteria for empirical legitimacy, on the other hand, are much less clear, and much more subject to disagreement among legitimacy theorists. At heart, the problem is that empirical legitimacy is a mental state, *inferred* from a range of opinions that people may express, few of which begin to approximate to the definition of normative legitimacy. Most citizens simply do not articulate views specifically about the legitimacy of the various authorities who require compliance of them. In relation to policing: they may say that they trust (or distrust) their local police (or their police force, detectives or traffic police); they may say that their police are competent; and they may think that they do (or do not) discriminate against particular groups. In the UK context, at least, holding attitudes of this sort can – as we shall see – be good *predictors* of conferring legitimacy on the police. However, does the espousal of such attitudes actually mean the same thing as conferring legitimacy on the police?

I would argue that it does not because it is more than conceivable that people may be staunch supporters of the police, and accept the legitimacy of their authority, in the full knowledge that they routinely act incompetently or unfairly, or breach other accepted standards of ethical and legal policing. When a person confers legitimacy on an authority, this involves two linked – and much narrower – mental states: first, the person has a sense of *obligation to obey* that authority; and, second, they have a sense of *shared moral values* with the authority, which generates a sense of obligation. What I mean by these two mental states of obligation to obey and moral alignment is best illustrated by the sorts of questions that we have used in survey research to measure them (see Box 2.1).

When we designed the large-scale test of the links between (empirical) legitimacy and compliance with the law using the European Social Survey (ESS) outlined in Box 2.1, we originally followed David Beetham's (1991) well-established definition of legitimacy, which proposes that power-holders command legitimacy when three conditions are met: the 'governed' offer their willing consent to defer to the authority; this consent is grounded on a degree of 'moral alignment' between the power-holder and the governed, as reflected in shared moral values; and the authority's actions conform to standards of legality (acting according to the law). We therefore

Box 2.1 Some survey questions used to measure empirical legitimacy

Sense of obligation to obey the police

Now some questions about your duty towards the police in this country. To what extent is it your duty to ...

- back the decisions made by the police even when you disagree with them?
- do what the police tell you even if you don't understand or agree with the reasons?
- do what the police tell you to do, even if you don't like how they treat you?

Response options: 11-point scale where 0 is 'not at all your duty' and 10 is 'completely your duty'.

Sense of moral alignment with the police

Please say to what extent you agree or disagree with each of the following statements about the police in this country:

- The police generally have the same sense of right and wrong as I do.
- The police stand up for values that are important to people like me.
- I generally support how the police usually act.

Response options: Agree strongly, agree, neither agree nor disagree, disagree, and disagree strongly.

Source: Round 5 of European Social Survey (see: www.europeansocialsurvey.org)

initially conceptualised (empirical) legitimacy as comprising *three* linked mental states: a sense of moral obligation to obey the authority; a sense of shared moral values with the authority; and a belief that the authority acted lawfully and 'played by the rules'. Conceptual analysis suggests that 'playing by the rules' is better seen as a dimension of procedural justice, rather than of legitimacy; adherence to legality *may* be a precondition for building legitimacy but one can envisage how a police officer might command legitimacy while bending or breaking rules and regulations. However, it is clear that beliefs about shared moral values and those about police lawfulness are closely correlated, at least in European settings.[12] (I shall summarise ESS findings in Chapter Three.)

It is important to stress that the normatively grounded sense of obligation – or duty – to obey the police that exists when people confer legitimacy on them is derived from their sense of moral alignment with the police. This is a very different sense of obligation to that which people feel when confronted with coercive force: the prudential obligation to comply with police demands when the alternative is likely to be arrest, charge and conviction. Faced with coercive force, people may certainly feel a *prudential* obligation to do what is demanded of them by other people but not a *moral duty* to do so.[13]

What creates and shapes empirical legitimacy?

Several different sorts of factors are likely to shape the levels of legitimacy that people confer on the police. There are three main sets of factors, though I would not suggest that these are exhaustive.

Early socialisation

Undoubtedly, for some, orientation towards the police evolves from early upbringing, where learning about right and wrong include concepts of crime and punishment. For most of us, the moral norms that are inculcated into us as children are graduated, differentiating between actions that are simply bad manners or rude, those that are clearly wrong, and those that are very wrong and often criminal. Fairness is a foundational concept in the acquisition of moral norms, and children start to acquire a sense of fairness from a very early age,[14] with an understanding that the police deal with unfair actions that are 'very bad indeed'.

It would be surprising if our moral education in childhood did not lay the groundwork for our orientation towards the police.[15]

Trust in the police

As people enter adolescence and early adulthood, they usually acquire more direct experience of the police, which is likely to play a much more formative part in shaping their sense of police legitimacy. So too is the indirect experience garnered through accounts of police contacts from family, friends, workmates and acquaintances. Accounts of police behaviour that people read or hear in the media are also likely to play a part, though probably less than the lived experience – whether direct or indirect – of contact with the police. Experience of this sort is likely to be translated into trust – or distrust – in the police. Trust is best envisaged as something that flows from the expectations that people hold about the future behaviour of others that will lead them to *entrust* their well-being to those people. For me to trust someone (or some institution) is to be prepared to place in their hands valued assets, such as my security, freedom or possessions, on the basis of a belief that that person is well intentioned towards me and competent to deliver on what I trust them to do.

In the context of the police (and other legal authorities), it is helpful to identify four key sorts of trust:

- trust in procedural fairness;
- trust in distributive fairness;
- trust in fair outcomes; and
- trust in competence.

Procedural justice theorists have argued that people's judgements about police procedural fairness are a critical determinant of the legitimacy that they confer on the police. Procedural fairness relates both to the integrity of the rules followed by the police and to the quality of treatment that the public receive from the police. Procedural fairness requires that the police: treat people with dignity and respect; explain the reasons for their actions when they have contact; listen to and take fully into account what people have to tell them; and 'play by the rules'.

Trust in distributive fairness relates to expectations that the police will treat different social groups equally, and will not discriminate against any group. Social groups that are often regarded as vulnerable to police discrimination include people from ethnic minority groups, people with 'alternative' lifestyles and people with stigmatised sexual preferences. Sometimes, groups may recognise police discrimination but see themselves as the *beneficiaries* of this discrimination. These people will not necessarily withdraw their support for the police as a consequence, and some might indeed welcome it. However, the impact on police legitimacy among those who are (or feel) *discriminated against* has the potential to be seriously negative. Arguably, legitimacy theorists have paid insufficient attention to trust in distributive fairness as a determinant of empirical legitimacy among minority groups – though in their defence, it could be argued that distributive fairness is simply a subcategory of procedural fairness.

Whatever the case, some of the post-war riots in England, notably, one in Brixton, South London, in 1981, had a racialised quality to them: many of the rioters were black and the triggers for the events were often grievances about the quality of policing among minority ethnic groups. The immediate problems underlying the Brixton riots were seen as an interaction between intense levels of social deprivation and a history of unlawful policing methods, racially prejudiced police conduct and the lack of consultation between police and community groups.[16] At the time, there was considerable public anxiety about street mugging and the police were thought to have responded with the indiscriminate overuse of stop-and-search tactics.

Trust in outcome fairness relates to expectations that police decisions result in fair outcomes. Outcomes may include decisions to arrest, to initiate prosecution, to warn formally or to take no formal action. A central claim of procedural justice theory is that procedural fairness is a much more significant determinant of legitimacy in the eyes of the public than outcome fairness, and that people will tolerate outcomes that are not in their personal best interests provided that they are treated with procedural fairness. As will be discussed in Chapter Three, there is a significant body of research to support this position.

A sceptic might argue that procedural fairness necessarily results in outcome fairness. However, this ignores the role of judgement and discretion in reaching fair outcomes: police officers often have to make judgement calls about the rights and wrongs of incidents to which they have been called, as well as the best response to these incidents, and different decisions can still be fairly reached in very similar situations.

Finally, trust in competence is an obvious precondition for people to confer legitimacy on the police. Here, competence ranges from quite simple things – actually answering calls for help, turning up on time or ensuring that commitments are fully met – to the performance of much more complex tasks, such as the sifting and presenting of evidence in criminal cases, the handling of public order events, the policing of terrorism, and dealing with highly vulnerable people. In affluent industrialised countries, it is easy to take for granted a basic level of police competence and thus overlook its importance in shaping legitimacy. However, there is some evidence (discussed in Chapter Three) that trust in competence can be a more significant determinant of legitimacy in developing countries with fewer resources to commit to policing. Where police forces lack the resources to achieve a basic level of competence, the role of (perceived) fairness in shaping legitimacy may be only subsidiary.

I should mention that there is a lively academic debate about the meaning and measurement of the concept of empirical legitimacy, and some scholars would disagree with the position taken here. Notably, some have argued that these forms of trust and perceptions of legality are *constituents* of empirical legitimacy rather than precursors or predictors of legitimacy.[17] In other words, they assume that if citizens confer (empirical) legitimacy on the police, they must necessarily – rather than simply contingently – regard the police as procedurally just, distributively just, lawful and effective. This is in contrast to the position that I take in this book, in common with my colleagues Jon Jackson and Ben Bradford (Jackson, 2018; Jackson and Bradford, 2019; Bradford, 2020). We have argued that perceptions of trust and of legality *predict* empirical legitimacy but that these forms of trust are *conceptually distinct* from empirical legitimacy. The ground that is shared by the two sides is much more significant than the definitional differences about which we have argued.

Social justice and political economy

The police inescapably form part of the state, and are, in the eyes of most citizens, representative – to some extent – of the state. In varying degrees, they represent (or symbolise) both the law and the government. Their legitimacy is thus inevitably and inextricably linked to judicial and political legitimacy. This poses the question of whether the police can ever hope to establish their legitimacy within a political system that itself lacks legitimacy. There is also the more complex question of whether in political systems that enjoy high levels of popular support, the police can simply feed off this political legitimacy.

The relationships between the police and the state exist at many levels. When the police come into direct conflict with the public over disorder arising from demonstrations and strikes, there is a clear risk to their legitimacy in the eyes of the policed. This risk is greatest when the police are using powers that are themselves contentious, or are acting as 'instruments of the state' in putting into effect contentious political policies. Perhaps the policing of the miners' strike in 1984/85, in particular, the 'Battle of Orgreave', is the clearest example of this in post-war Britain. The police were clearly aligned with, and instruments of, a Thatcherite government policy to break the power of the trade unions. There are, of course, two sides to this story; however, there can be little doubt that police legitimacy suffered badly in mining communities and beyond as a result. At Orgreave, 71 striking miners were charged with riot and 24 with violent disorder. The police evidence in court was ruled unreliable.[18]

Even when the police are not engaged in such problematic forms of policing, they are, to an extent, necessarily symbols of the state. Thus, there is also likely to be a diffuse and complex relationship between perceptions of social and economic justice and the perceived legitimacy of the police. Where income inequality is intense and social mobility is limited, those social groups that are locked into relative disadvantage are unlikely to confer legitimacy on those institutions that serve to maintain the status quo. Other things being equal, they are less likely than others to offer their consent to the rule of law, and more likely to attract the attention of the police. Disentangling the forms of distributive injustice that expose them to risks of deprivation, risks of involvement in crime and risks of unwanted police attention is both technically challenging and politically contentious.[19]

There is growing evidence that there are connections between income inequalities in any given country and its citizens' attachment to – or detachment from – social norms. That income inequalities damage the well-being of citizens is increasingly well established. Although controversial and much critiqued,[20] Wilkinson and Pickett's (2009) book *The Spirit Level* marshals an impressive volume of cross-national and time-series evidence about correlations between income inequality and a wide range of social ills. The authors do not offer an extensive explanation of *why* high levels of inequality should lead to crime, though the obvious candidates are the criminogenic nature of unmet basic needs – in relation to absolute deprivation – and the sense of unfairness suffered by those who are victims of extreme relative deprivation. Their explanations focus on the lack of respect and sense of resentment experienced by those at the bottom of the income ladder.

A more elaborate explanation can be found in theories of institutional anomie (IAT),[21] which work as a useful counterpoint at a societal level to the individual and organisational focus of procedural justice theory. According to these theories, societies that are committed to the goal of material success and that celebrate economic competition as the best way of ensuring material success may be corrosive of normative systems of social control embedded in institutions such as the family, the educational system and religions. More specific claims of IAT are that *rapid transitions* in society towards the values of free-market economies – which privilege competition over cooperation – can unbalance and weaken traditional normative systems of social control. Put crudely, neo-liberal economic policy, with its emphasis on the need for marketplace competition, may generate crime.[22]

I have not set out here to identify *all* the possible factors that shape police legitimacy in the eyes of the policed. What is clear,

I hope, is that police do not have full control over the levels of legitimacy that they can command. Sources of legitimacy are to be found not only in what the police do and how they do it, but also in the ways in which we are variously brought up as moral beings, and the ways in which we experience broader forms of social justice (or injustice).

Without doubt, there are many other factors – cultural, religious and historical – that are at play, and it is important to be sensitive to the risks of ethnocentrism in how we think about the legitimacy of authorities. In common with most criminologists with an interest in theories of legitimacy, I am preoccupied with the ways in which the police in developed, Western, industrialised democracies retain or lose their legitimacy. The more that societies elsewhere diverge from our own, the smaller the likelihood is that the analysis of policing offered here will be fully applicable to them. The ways in which the legitimacy of rigid theocracies was historically sustained, for example, probably bears little resemblance to the processes at work in contemporary Western democracies. Furthermore, without doubt, single-party states at some stages of their evolution sometimes manage to capture extreme levels of loyalty and affection from the governed in ways that are often absent from contemporary Western democracies. It has also been argued – convincingly to my mind – that within different cultures, there are embedded deeply differing conceptions of the individual's relationship to society and of the nature of moral obligation.[23] One should guard against assuming that procedural justice theory, developed in Western industrialised democracies, is universally applicable – or, indeed, universally appropriate.

The consequences of legitimacy: compliance and cooperation

It scarcely needs repeating that transforming coercive power into legitimate authority is a highly desirable goal for power-holders in straightforwardly instrumental terms because this generates compliance and cooperation on the part of those who are subject to authority. Other things being equal, engendering among the governed a morally grounded sense of obligation to obey the authority will result in compliance with the law. By the same token, a legitimate authority can expect to secure a dividend in terms of public cooperation – in reporting crimes and other issues, in acting as witnesses, and in providing information to the police. This is not a new idea, of course. Securing consent to the rule of law has been a principle of British policing to greater or lesser degree since the establishment of the Metropolitan Police in 1829. In the context of securing public order in colonial contexts, 'winning hearts and minds' has been a principle of both policing and military rule even if hard policing tactics were often deployed.[24]

The value of legitimating power has generally been accepted as simple common sense: improving police–community relations should, as a matter of course, have value in preventing crime. At best, there has been a loosely articulated assumption that good relations between the police and the public will yield cooperation and compliance with the law, based on somewhat truistic principles of reciprocation or mutual self-interest. However, over the last two decades, legitimacy research has offered a much richer understanding of the ways in which police power is legitimated. Collectively, this work shines a light on the processes of legitimation, as well as on the causal mechanisms that energise these essentially normative processes.

Compliance, defiance and hard power traps

The day-to-day pressures on police officers can also work against principles of procedural justice. It is easy to maintain standards of politeness and civility when dealing with tractable and compliant citizens. It is much harder to do so when – as often happens – people challenge police authority and refuse to comply with officers' demands. Faced with such challenges, officers can respond in several ways. The worst choices are probably to withdraw or cave in, and to make no further demands for compliance. These are bad choices because they squander officers' authority – at least in that encounter and in any future encounters with the same people. Another option is to overwhelm the challenge with coercive force – most obviously, through arrest. This is the most tempting response to challenge, being an instinctive way of dealing both with disrespect and with the potential threat to personal safety that is inherent in challenges to police authority. However, the best response – if it can be achieved – is to use procedural justice tactics to de-escalate the challenge and to secure compliance without coercion. Political scientists often draw a distinction between soft power and hard power.[25] Hard power involves the use of coercion by one state against another, while soft power, or co-optive power, is where one state deploys forms of persuasion and encouragement, underpinned by moral authority, to get other states to want the same outcomes as itself. European countries, notably, the UK and France, have tended to be leaders in the use of soft power, as measured by the 'Soft Power 30' index,[26] with Russia and Turkey currently occupying the bottom two places. The distinction has limitations in the analysis of statecraft,[27] but in the policing context, it neatly captures the distinctions between coercive power and the use of legitimate authority.

Most of us respond prudentially to hard power threats but some people do not, especially when the threats are made in ways that are disrespectful. They place greater importance on challenging the lack of respect than on avoiding the consequences of non-compliance. The more extensive experience that people have of disrespectful police treatment, and the more that this is a collective experience, the more likely they are to respond with defiance than compliance.[28] More problematic still, past experience may make them anticipate disrespectful treatment, or interpret police actions as disrespectful, regardless of any police intent. This dynamic creates the risk of a 'hard power trap' for the police, where the only strategies that remain open to them are ones that involve coercive force. Once abrasive tactics have been overused, and trust has been lost, persuasive soft power tactics may no longer have any purchase on the policed population. Rowing back from the overuse of hard power is a significant challenge in the policing of some communities, discussed further in Chapters Four and Five.

There are many situations where hard power tactics are the only ones that are appropriate. When people are determined to resist arrest, for example, or when their behaviour poses serious dangers to themselves or others, deploying overwhelming coercive force may simply be unavoidable. It must also be recognised that many of those who are deeply entangled with the criminal law have lifelong histories of resistance to authority of all sorts, for example, parental and school authority, as well as control by social workers, social care staff and youth justice workers. Where their response to police demands is one of defiance, coercive force may again be a necessity. However, at the same time, the skilled deployment of soft power tactics may successfully head off defiant responses.

Towards a definition of good policing

There are many dimensions to good policing as police organisations are complex and multifunctional. For example, the police can be good or bad at finding, marshalling and presenting evidence in court. They may, or may not, handle public order events successfully. They may treat people with mental health issues well or badly. Their ability to respond to terrorist threats may vary. Their performance can differ on these and many other dimensions. However, it may be helpful to frame a definition of good policing at the most general of levels in order to provide an overarching framework within which performance can be assessed across a wide range of functions. Using the perspective advocated in this book, I would argue that good policing involves striking the best possible balance between hard and soft policing, in ways that maximise police legitimacy. Good policing necessarily involves the use of coercive force in some situations but strives to minimise its use. A central criterion in assessing the quality of policing should always be whether it enhances or reduces police legitimacy.

This definition of good policing can be justified on both practical and political grounds. In practical terms, policing that maximises legitimacy produces the outcomes that any police organisation should welcome: public compliance with the law and public cooperation. Moreover, as I have argued, the normative compliance that fair policing engenders is more stable, and more economical, than policing that keeps the population in a firm deterrent grip.

Procedural justice theorists have usually focused on these practical benefits in arguing their case – presumably to capture the attention of those whose natural instinct is for firm deterrent crime-fighting strategies. However, the value of fostering police legitimacy and thus securing consent to the rule of law can be justified more securely on political grounds, or, more accurately, on political ethics grounds. The argument is simply that it is a measure of a good state that it should treat its citizens with dignity, fairness and respect, and that state bureaucracies should be responsible for ensuring that this happens. In other words, the definition of good policing that I am proposing delivers both practical and ethico-political benefits.

I would not claim any originality in the sort of definition that I have set out. The body of work by Tom Tyler and colleagues implicitly – and sometimes explicitly – makes the same case. For example, Tracey Meares (2013) put forward a similar argument for treating procedural fairness as the first requirement of policing. She argued that the two dominant – and competing – ways of evaluating police performance have traditionally been legality and effectiveness, and that neither of these is adequate by itself. She proposed that a third evaluative criterion should be foregrounded: that of 'rightful policing', defined as procedurally fair policing. Meares served as one of the members of President Obama's Task Force into Policing for the 21st Century, a quote from which opened this chapter. The quotation made the striking statement that procedural justice should be the guiding principle of policing policy and practice.

If I have sketched out what I regard as a cogent – if very general – test of good *policing*, it follows that a good police officer is someone who is skilled at handling authority and takes care to squander neither their personal legitimacy nor that of their organisation. Thus, a good *police officer* is someone who treats those with whom they have contact fairly and respectfully, accords them dignity, and listens to what they have to say. However, this raises the question of whether good police officers simply have to *perform* fairness and respect, or whether they are required to hold and internalise the values that underpin legitimate policing. The answer to this question is a complex one that goes to the heart of the nature of the police occupation. Does policing require of its practitioners the development of a moral perspective that results in a sympathetic appreciation of human frailty,[29] or does it simply demand the straightforward honing of 'people skills' to get the job done? We shall return to this question at the end of the book.

Conclusions

This chapter has set out the conceptual framework that underpins the book's arguments. Police legitimacy, seen through the eyes of the policed, provides the foundation of good policing. While many different factors can shape the degree of legitimacy that people confer on the police, policing styles – *how* the police go about their work – matter a great deal. The surest route to building police legitimacy is for officers to act with procedural fairness. People value being treated with dignity and respect; they expect and want to be listened to, and to be given explanations for police actions; and they expect the police to act fairly and to 'play by the rules'. The more that the police achieve this, the stronger the sense of identification will be between the police and the policed, and the more that people will feel that the police share their values and have their best interests at heart. That lays the foundation for a solid, normatively grounded, commitment to the rule of law.

3

The evidence: the power of fairness

This chapter summarises some of the research that supports the book's principal argument that legitimacy is central to effective policing, and that policing policy and practice need to keep a sharp focus on factors that build or destroy police legitimacy. The chapter does not set out to provide a comprehensive survey of the literature as other reviews are available.[1] Rather, I shall try to give a flavour of the research, drawing mainly on international surveys that I and colleagues have carried out. I shall also summarise research that provides explanations for the importance that we all attach to fair treatment from those who exercise power over us.

The evidence about procedural fairness is largely quantitative, using surveys, and there is a dearth of detailed qualitative work. Surveys necessarily offer a simplified version of the complexities of the real world. To emphasise this, the chapter starts with an extract from field notes for a qualitative, observational study[2] that illustrates the real-world dilemmas facing patrol officers who are at risk of finding themselves in hard power traps (see Box 3.1). I hope the field notes speak for themselves.

Surveys of trust, legitimacy and compliance

In aggregate, the evidence supporting the approach for which I argue is strong but not beyond question. Evidence about the best ways of making people behave well is rarely clinching because the relevant research has to grapple with human behaviour at its most complex. I offer my own assessment of

---

Box 3.1 Who owns the streets? Police versus young people in an inner-city area

17.45 I am with two officers in an unmarked police car patrolling a busy area. We drive past a row of shops and the officers point out a group of seven young people hanging around outside the newsagent. One says that the colours they are wearing signify they are members of a particular 'crew'. The officers tell me that although the crew has been quiet for some time, it is known for violence and drug dealing. They circle the area and drive past again; one of the boys waves at the officers. The officers contact their colleagues and ask to meet them so they can discuss what to do. They meet and decide to search the group to see if they are carrying anything.

They decide to surprise them – so they cannot run away – and approach from different directions. There are five officers in two cars. They approach from different directions, jump out of the cars and surround the young people. All of them are mixed race boys under the age of 17. They do not try to walk away but look bemused. At the kerbside is a car with one of their friends in it, a young mixed-race woman, with her toddler. The officers tell the group that they are going to be searched. Within five minutes, the encounter has attracted considerable attention from passers-by. Some of these people question the police about their tactics and accuse them of being heavy-handed.

The teenagers stay fairly calm but say they do not think the police have the grounds to search them, complaining that they have not been told of the grounds of the search. An officer tells them they are being searched because they are known gang members. One of the boys goes right up to an officer with his face a couple of inches from the officer's face, and laughs at him, telling him he has no idea what goes on in the streets. The officer tries to ignore him. After the teenager has been searched, he moves over to the car and turns the volume up on the stereo. He then returns to where one of the officers is standing and starts to dance around him, keeping his face only inches away from the officer's face at all times. The officer stands his ground and says nothing. Some of the crowd are cheering the young man on and his friends laugh at the scene unfolding before them. One of them shouts to his friend: 'He can't do nothin' as he knows this is our manor and there is too many watching his every move, he's fucked, man, and he knows it – the pain for him, you'll pay for it the next time he sees you on your own.'

After we leave the area, the officers discuss how difficult it is to police young people in their area. One of the officers says that most of the local residents can't decide how they want the police to behave. He believes that in this area, there is only one appropriate style of policing and that is aggressive. He further comments that whatever style of policing they adopt, it will never be right. 'We just have to accept that here we will never be in the right, or liked. We are damned if we do a lot of searches and damned if we don't.' One of the officers comments that he would rather stop and search more young people and stretch the boundaries of reasonable suspicion than turn up at a parent's front door to tell them their child is either dead or in hospital. He then comments that the local residents need to decide what they want, aggressive policing that keeps kids alive or 'nicey nicey policing' and more dead or injured kids.

Source: May et al (2010: 41–43)

the quality of the evidence at the end of this chapter, and leave it to the reader to decide what weight to attach to it. However, it scarcely needs saying that I find it persuasive.

A large amount of survey research has established the existence of strong relationships between different types of fairness, perceptions of legitimacy, preparedness to comply with the law and preparedness to cooperate with law officers. I have been involved in several such surveys, two of which are large-scale comparative studies involving many countries. The first is the European Social Survey (ESS), which interviews over 50,000 adults in around 30 European countries every two years.[3] With colleagues, I designed a suite of questions on trust in justice and legitimacy that was included in the fifth round of the survey in 2010.[4]

The second survey is the third round of the International Self Report Delinquency Study (ISRD3), which again included questions on trust and legitimacy, similar to those used in the ESS. This interviewed almost 63,000 teenagers in 27 countries across the world.[5] The two surveys used similar strategies to examine trust in justice and legitimacy. They included various measures of trust in the police, measures of people's perceptions of legitimacy and measures of compliance with the law. They can thus be used to test whether the various relationships between trust, legitimacy and compliance predicted by procedural justice theory are actually found in the real world.

The ESS

The ESS measured the two dimensions of empirical legitimacy discussed in Chapter Two, as well as various dimensions of people's trust in the police (trust in competence, in procedural fairness and in distributive fairness). Figure 3.1 shows the percentages of respondents who thought that the police often or very often treat people with respect – one of the questions measuring trust in procedural fairness. It groups the 26 countries in our analysis into regions, and also includes findings on a comparable survey mounted at the same time by Japanese colleagues[6] that used the module of questions that we had devised for the ESS.

The findings show very marked differences between levels of trust across regions. Ex-communist countries in Eastern Europe score lowest, though Israel – which takes part in the ESS as an 'associated state' of the European Union – also scores badly. Scandinavian countries score highest, with the British Isles (the UK and the Republic of Ireland) not far behind.

Figure 3.2 shows similar findings for one of the items that measures perceptions of empirical legitimacy. People were asked to say how much they agreed with the statement 'To what extent is it your duty to do what the police tell you even if you don't understand or agree with the reasons?' The ordering of scores by region contains some surprises. Israelis score highest on this dimension of legitimacy, despite scoring low on ratings of procedural justice, and Japanese score lowest, despite the stereotypes that many Westerners hold of Japanese deference to authority. British and Irish people score quite low on ratings of legitimacy, even though they rate the police highly on respectful treatment. One can speculate on explanations for

Figure 3.1: Percentage saying that the police generally treat people with respect

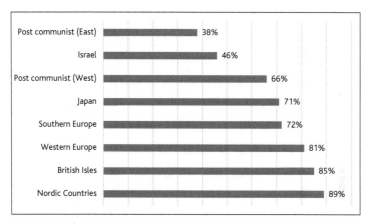

Notes: Post-communist (East) = Estonia, Russia and Ukraine; post-communist (West) = Bulgaria, Croatia, Czech Republic, Hungary, Poland, Slovakia and Slovenia; Southern European = Cyprus, Greece, Portugal and Spain; Western European = France, Belgium, Germany, Netherlands and Switzerland; Nordic countries = Denmark, Finland, Norway and Sweden; British Isles = England, Wales, Scotland, Northern Ireland and Republic of Ireland. Japan conducted a survey in parallel to the ESS (see Tsushima and Hamai, 2015). Wording: 'How often would you say the police generally treat people with respect?' Percentage saying 'often' or 'very often'.

Source: 2010 ESS

the anomalies. The sense of existential threat that many Israelis feel that their country is subject to may lead them to tolerate disrespectful treatment from the police, while conferring a very high level of legitimacy on the police. Moreover, the Japanese may confer low levels of legitimacy on the police precisely because their normative commitment to the rule of law is shaped by unrelated factors, making the police much more marginal to order maintenance than in the West.

For our purposes, the rank order of regions on trust and (empirical) legitimacy is less important than the strength of relationships that we find between trust, legitimacy and compliance. Table 3.1 summarises the predictive power of different types of trust on the level of legitimacy that people confer on the police. It summarises the results of fairly complex country-by-country statistical modelling, in which scales were constructed to measure:

Figure 3.2: Perceived legitimacy: obligation to obey

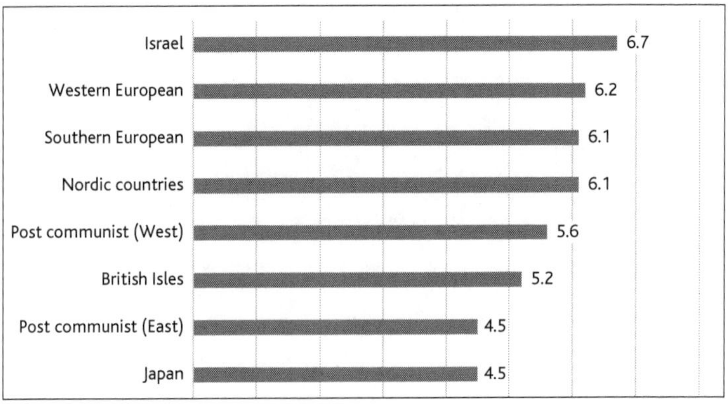

Notes: For the list of countries, see Figure 3.1. Wording: 'To what extent is it your duty to do what the police tell you even if you don't understand or agree with the reasons?' Scale: 0–10, running from 'not at all' to 'completely'. Scores are the average of responses. High scores indicate high sense of duty to obey the police.

Source: 2010 ESS

- three dimensions of trust (trust in effectiveness, in procedural fairness and in distributive fairness); and
- two dimensions of legitimacy (obligation to obey and moral alignment).

Table 3.1 shows that in all countries, trust in procedural fairness was a strong and statistically significant predictor of both the main dimension of legitimacy – people's sense that the police share their values – and the resultant sense of obligation that people have to obey the demands that the police make of them. Trust in police effectiveness was also predictive of both dimensions but not in every country, and not at the same level of statistical significance. These are important findings that many people may find counter-intuitive. They imply that when it comes to building police legitimacy, policing style – *how* the police do things – may be more important than *what* the police do. Being competent is important but not as important as treating people well.

We found much weaker relationships between trust in distributive fairness and legitimacy, which can be interpreted as reflecting the likelihood that most people will have little

Table 3.1: Relationships between the dimensions of trust and legitimacy across 26 countries

	Dimension 1 of legitimacy: moral alignment	Dimension 2 of legitimacy: felt obligation to obey
Trust in procedural fairness	✓✓✓	✓✓✓
Trust in distributive fairness	✓	✗
Trust in effectiveness	✓✓	✓✓

Note: Key: ✓✓✓ = strong predictor of legitimacy in all countries; ✓✓ = weak predictor of legitimacy in most countries; ✓ = weak predictor in under half of countries; and ✗ = weak predictor in very few countries.

Source: 2010 ESS (Hough et al, 2013)

direct experience bearing on the fact as to whether others receive worse – or better – police treatment than they do. As will be discussed in Chapter Four, this does not negate the possibility that distributive unfairness on the part of the police can play an important part in the social marginalisation of some minority groups.

The ESS covers a fairly homogeneous group of developed, industrialised countries, most of which have a commitment to democratic values and human rights. Being a survey of European countries, it can say nothing about other countries, notably, those in the Global South. There is some comparable evidence about the drivers of legitimacy in a few developing countries. For example, both in South Africa and Pakistan, trust in police effectiveness is a stronger predictor of legitimacy than trust in procedural fairness, at least for some groups. As Jon Jackson put it in an international review:

> Procedural justice is the strongest predictor of police legitimacy in most of the countries under investigation, although normative judgements about fair process may – in some contexts – be crowded out by public concerns about police effectiveness and corruption, the scale of the crime problem, and the association of the police with a historically oppressive and underperforming state.[7]

Jackson and colleagues have also documented the very complex relations between the police and the public in San Paulo, Brazil, where crime, fear of crime and fear of the police are all very high. They found that procedural justice yet again emerges as an important determinant of empirical legitimacy but that instrumental considerations – the need for protection and the fear of the police – shaped many people's sense of obligation to obey the police.[8]

Does the ESS show that conferring legitimacy on the police is associated with compliance with the law and preparedness to cooperate with the police? In other words, will trust-building strategies designed to consolidate police legitimacy result in public compliance with the law and cooperation with the police? The ESS offers a positive answer to these questions, even if the findings are less clear at present than those about the links between trust and legitimacy. Against various measures, a belief in police legitimacy predicts cooperation with the police (for example, Jackson et al, 2015). We also showed that in the UK, legitimacy predicts compliance with the law, where compliance is measured by a scale combining answers to questions asking respondents whether they had committed any of three offences in the previous five years. However, the quality of the relevant data was poor, and levels of admissions were implausibly low in many countries. Rather more robust findings emerged from the ISRD, to which we now turn.

The ISRD3

The ISRD3 was carried out in 27 countries, with most data collection taking place between 2014 and 2016. Young people aged 12 to 16 completed a school-based questionnaire asking a wide range of questions, including experience of crime as both victims and offenders, involvement in other risky behaviour such as alcohol and illicit drug use, and attitudes to, and experience of, the police. One set of questions was adapted from the ESS battery of questions on trust in justice and legitimacy, and, as in the ESS, we were able to test the relationships between trust in the police, perceived police legitimacy and compliance with the law. It is the first large-scale international test of procedural justice theory among teenagers, and its coverage of countries was broader than the ESS, including samples from the US and from the Global South.

Levels of trust (measured on a scale that largely reflected trust in procedural justice) were strongly predictive of assessments of police legitimacy in all 27 countries. In 18 out of the 27 countries, trust in the police was a statistically significant – and negative – predictor of preparedness to commit offences, and in most of these 18 countries, the predictive effect can be attributed to the perceived legitimacy in the police engendered by this trust.[9] The ISRD3 findings are important, in showing that across a wide range of different countries and cultures, the relationships predicted by procedural justice theory between trust in the police and perceptions of police legitimacy, and between legitimacy and involvement in crime, appear to hold among samples of teenagers at a point in their lives when their personal experience of the police is becoming significant.

Procedural justice and stop-and-search

A more detailed examination focusing on the English and Scottish samples of ISRD3 can provide a bit more texture to these results.[10] The background is that in the five years leading up to the time of fieldwork, England and Scotland had created a 'natural experiment' in the use of stop-and-search. In England, following pressure from then Home Secretary Theresa May and HMICFRS (the national police inspectorate), police forces south of the border were using stop-and-search *less* than previously, and using it with more care. In Scotland, on the other hand, Police Scotland was engaged in an explicit policy of making *greater* use of the tactic.

Consistent with other ISRD3 countries, ISRD3 showed that trust in the police predicted perceived legitimacy and both trust in the police and perceived legitimacy were significant (negative) predictors of (self-reported) offending. The UK sample also collected information on teenagers' experience of police stop-and-search, and analysis showed that experience of stop-and-search appeared to depress levels of trust and perceptions of legitimacy. The findings clearly suggest that the higher usage of stop-and-search tactics in Scotland could account for lower levels of trust and legitimacy in that country, and could be counterproductive in resulting in lower compliance with the law.

This is not to say that all use of stop-and-search damages the trust of those who are searched, and research from the US shows that stop-and-search can be conducted in a procedurally fair way. Illustrating this, Box 3.2 contains a further extract from field notes from our qualitative study. However, an important set of findings, mainly from the US, has shown that the impact of good and bad experiences of the police on people's trust in them is asymmetrical,[11] that is, bad experiences depress trust in the police much more than good experiences build trust. As the Dutch proverb has it: 'Trust arrives on foot but leaves on horseback.' Every encounter between the police and the public is potentially a 'teachable moment', where the costs of the wrong lesson are high.

Experimental research

So far, I have presented the results of snapshot surveys, which capture people's attitudes and experiences at a single moment in time. These surveys are poorly placed to attribute cause and effect.[12] However, there are a few randomised controlled trials (and related quasi-experimental evaluations), some of which offer good support for the effectiveness of interventions grounded in procedural justice theory (for example, Mazerolle et al, 2013). These have involved the experimental manipulation of the procedural fairness of contacts with the public and assessing the impact this has on measures of trust and legitimacy. Thus, Mazerolle and colleagues divided Australian traffic police into teams that either conducted driver breath tests as normal or else carried out the breath test following a specially devised script that contained more salient elements of procedural fairness. In a follow-up survey the experimental group expressed more positive attitudes to the police.[13] Clearly, more studies of this sort are needed.

Box 3.2 A well-handled stop-and-search

17.45 The officers I am observing are driving through a well-known open drug market when they spot a teenager down an alleyway with a bike appearing to fiddle with his sock while talking to a white girl. The two officers believe that the boy may be selling drugs. One of the officers jumps out of the car to see what is going on. He approaches the two and startles them. He asks what they are doing, the boy replies: 'I'm chatting to my friend.' The officer asks how old he is and if he has anything on him he shouldn't. He replies that he is 16 and he doesn't have anything on him. The girl doesn't reply. The officer tells the boy that he is in an area known for drug selling and that he is down an alley fiddling with his sock and hence he is going to search him for drugs. The boy is taken aback and tells the officer he was tying his shoelace. He appears put out by the intrusion and asks the officer if he is being searched because he is black. The officer reiterates what he has said earlier, adding that when he saw the two, he didn't know what ethnicity they were. The officer carries out the search, nothing is found and the checks come back negative. The officer apologises to the young man for keeping him and asks if he wants a copy of the stop-and-search form. He informs him that the form will be kept back at the police station if he decides he wants it at a later date. The boy decides not to wait for the form. The officer apologises again, and jokes that he can sometimes jump to conclusions about young people in alleyways. The young man accepts his apology and leaves with his friend.

Source: May et al (2010: 47–48)

Why is procedural justice so important?

Insofar as fair outcomes generate trust and build legitimacy, it is not hard to find explanations for this. People simply want to see fair play. It is less obvious why people attach so much importance to procedural fairness, in particular, to the quality of personal treatment that they and others receive from authority figures. Why do many of us – perhaps the majority – place greater value on being treated with dignity and respect by a police officer than by a customs officer, ticket inspector or traffic warden? Part of the explanation is that we have simply been brought up to expect power-holders to treat people well, and that this expectation increases with the level of power that power-holders exercise.[14] Being treated by a police officer with respect and politeness, being given an opportunity to explain what is going on, being listened to, and being treated with dignity – these all signal important things about one's social position, precisely because of the police officer's position as a representative of state power.

It is obvious that when people are seeking help from the police, they will value fair and respectful treatment. It is less obvious that when people are approached by the police as suspects – an inherently disrespectful process – they can accept the process as legitimate if they are given reasons for the contact, if their explanations are listened to and if the police handle the contact with tact and politeness. A contact of this quality can signal simultaneously that the suspect deserves dignified and respectful treatment as a *citizen* even if action has to be taken against them if they have committed an offence. It would be naive to propose that principles of procedural justice can always stop contacts between the police and the public spiralling into conflict. However, it should be clear that procedural *injustice* can rapidly inflame difficult situations, and is never likely to help resolve them.

Chapter Two discussed how childhood socialisation laid the foundations for our expectations of fair treatment. One reason why people value procedural fairness so much in their contact with the police is to be found in childhood and adolescent socialisation, which takes place in the family, in schools, among friends and – where things go wrong – in the justice system.[15] Expectations of fair play, decent treatment and a degree of understanding on the part of authority figures are inculcated into children from an early age, and this extends to expectations about the police. However, when people are in contact with the police, receiving fair (or unfair) treatment may also signify particular things about their standing or status, or their belonging to (or exclusion from) social groups, and represent a challenge to their social identity.

People's social identity is their sense of who they are, derived from their sense of the social groups with which they identify or feel membership. People often see themselves as being members of multiple groups; they may feel themselves to be British, for example, belonging to a particular social class, to an ethnic group, to an occupational group, to friendship or family networks, and so on.[16] Group membership is a source of self-esteem and well-being, and having a sense of exclusion from a group can damage one's sense of self-worth. The police are often seen as representing significant and dominant social groups, and being treated by the police in ways that are seen to be unfair is damaging to those who see the police as representing dominant social values. Ben Bradford (2020) puts this well:

> The experience of procedurally *just* policing strengthens the bonds between the individual and this superordinate group, while procedural injustice denigrates, marginalizes and excludes. By and through the ways in which they treat people officers can generate, encourage or enhance a sense of inclusion and value within the group, and promote identification with police as a source of authority and with the values the institution of police is intended to represent. The strengthening of bonds with the group, and with police as its representatives, in turn enhances trust, legitimacy, cooperation and compliance. (Emphasis in original)

One can speculate that those whose social identity is particularly fragile may react more strongly than others when exposed to forms of injustice that challenge their sense of belonging.[17]

Earlier in this chapter we presented an extract from field notes for a study comparing different styles of policing. It described a well-conducted stop-and-search in a police division that followed standards of procedural justice. The extract in Box 3.3 from the same study describes a stop-and-search in a division where officers were much more concerned with demonstrating control on the streets. No explanation was offered for the stop, which was conducted with minimum respect and with no sign of an apology when nothing was discovered.

Box 3.3 A stop-and-search failing to meet standards of procedural justice

17.30 The officers I am with receive intelligence of a sighting of a prominent gang member thought to be carrying a gun. The officers drive to areas frequented by gang members. We see three black teenagers (two aged 17 and one aged 19) on the street and follow them. The officers tell me that these are not associated with the gang they are concerned with but think it prudent to stop and search them as they are 'walking together at a strange time of the day'. [It was unclear to the researcher what was strange about the time of day.]

They pull over to talk to the three boys, who stop and immediately begin to shake their heads. The officers tell them to stand against a nearby wall, and they call for back-up. Shortly thereafter four officers arrive in two marked cars. The teenagers are searched. Each of them complies with the officers' requests. It is clear that they don't know the reasons for the stop. They repeatedly ask the officers why they have been stopped, who respond by saying that they have the powers to do so. At no stage are the young men told why they have been stopped. However, the officers tell me later that it is because they matched the description of the gang member who they thought was in possession of a gun.

The teenagers are obviously unhappy about the search. However, two of the three remain calm and say nothing. The third is upset and angry. He persistently asks the officers to explain why he has been stopped and makes many comments about the police 'always being on the back of black men'. He protests that all he and his friends were doing was walking along the road and asks the officers how this can be regarded as criminal behaviour. One of the officers says that the way he was walking looked 'dodgy', and asks why he and his friends were out and about at this time. This infuriates the young man.

While waiting for the checks, one of the officers photographs the teenagers. The three ask why they are being photographed and the officer informs them that he has the permission of his superintendent to take photographs of all those who are stopped and searched. They are told that their photos may be used for the purposes of intelligence and will be deleted within seven days if they are not required. They are angered by this, in part because they are asked to remove their headgear. The checks reveal that both 17-year-olds are known to the police but they are not currently wanted. The outcome is 'no further action'. The most vocal of the three asks for a copy of the stop and search form, which at the time has not been started. The officer remarks that the completion of the form could take anywhere between 15 to 20 minutes as his 'writing hand hurts and so it's a little slow today'. The teenager confirms that he is happy to wait and demands that a form be completed. His two friends are laughing and tell him to forget about the form so that they can be on their way. He is adamant, however, that he wants a copy.

While waiting, the young man tells his friends that he is in court the following day and will produce this and the other forms to show the judge that he is frequently stopped and searched by the police. The officers ask why he is attending court, and he tells them to mind their own business. He does, however, inform them that he will be appearing before the youth court. The officers laugh and tell him that 'the youth court is for kids' and how he isn't a real man yet because if he was, he would be at the Crown Court. The young male retaliates by swearing at the officers. His friends, who are both laughing, tell him to shut up and impress upon him that the officers are winding him up for the fun of it and he should keep quiet. After some time, the officer provides the young man with a stop and search form and they depart the scene.

Source: May et al (2010: 46–47)

Assessing the evidence

This chapter has given only an indication of the research evidence in support of the ideas presented in this book. There are many other studies of policing and the courts, most of which have been carried out in Europe, North America and Australia, reaching similar conclusions. There is also a much broader evidence base about the importance of organisational justice in the workplace (discussed in Chapter Five) which lends additional support to the idea that people are very responsive to procedural fairness in a range of settings. However, overall, the research evidence is persuasive that the fair treatment of people by power-holders legitimates their authority, and that this legitimacy generates compliance. It would be wrong to suggest that the available evidence is clinching[18] in proving *beyond doubt* that the claimed relationships exist, and the limitations of the evidence base need to be stated. Research rarely achieves this level of certainty when evaluating complex theories about social behaviour.

Most of the evidence is based on snapshot surveys. These surveys demonstrate beyond doubt that associations (or statistical correlations) exist between trust, legitimacy and compliance at a single point in time; however, as I have suggested, they cannot establish the direction of causality that the theory implies. Some critics have argued that the causal direction is actually in the opposite direction to that proposed by procedural justice theorists; in other words, non-compliance with the law is a precursor of low ratings of police legitimacy and low trust in the police. There are two legs to the argument. First, critics appeal to psychological theories such as cognitive dissonance theory, which suggest that people adjust their attitudes to be consistent with their behaviour. If they have been drawn into criminal behaviour, they may adopt more negative attitudes to the law and the police to justify their behaviour. Conversely, if they accept social rules and the laws that underpin them, they are unlikely to hold very negative views about the institutions that support these rules and laws. Second, the more that people engage in lawbreaking, the more they will risk attracting police attention, and their contacts with the police may well be negative and erode whatever trust they might have in the police.

System justification theory also provides a significant elaboration of, or qualification to, procedural justice theory. Political psychologists (for example, Jost et al, 2010) have proposed that people feel under pressure to justify the social order of which they are part, and that this process affects not only those who are the greatest beneficiaries of the status quo, but also, paradoxically, those who are treated least fairly. The argument is that people are motivated to believe that the social system that regulates their lives is appropriate and proper because this provides the most comfortable accommodation with any social injustices to which they are exposed. System justification theory represents a challenge to procedural justice theory's central claim that power-holders need to *earn* their legitimacy because – the argument goes – people confer legitimacy on that system, at least in part, *because* it can exercise authority over them (Jost et al, 2010; see also Lukes, 2005). I shall return to system justification theory in Chapter Six because it is also relevant to the argument that procedural justice approaches can provide a palliative to the experience of unjust power.

The likely resolution to these debates is to recognise that there is a complex and interactive dynamic between orientations to the police, experiences of the police and engagement in crime. Attitudes shape behaviour, and behaviour shapes attitudes. What is needed is more longitudinal survey work tracing the development of attitudes over time, more experimental work testing causal mechanisms and more qualitative research to sit beside the survey data, examining the micro-dynamics of contacts with the police.[19]

Nor should the explanatory reach of procedural justice theory be overstated. While we can readily accept that most people are guided most of the time by some normative principles, we really are rational calculators of costs and benefits – the *homo economicus* of classic economic theory – in some aspects of our lives. Regulatory offences such as exceeding vehicle speed limits provide us with an obvious example of deterrence theory in action, with the probability of sanction being self-evidently important and legitimacy serving only as a marginal shaping consideration (but see Bradford et al, 2015). Often, the most parsimonious – and much ignored – explanation for compliance is simply habit.[20]

There is certainly scope for more conceptual and empirical work in both the definition of legitimacy and the identification of the key 'drivers' of legitimacy. As discussed, the boundaries between the concepts of trust and legitimacy are drawn in different ways by different scholars, and the constituent elements of subjective legitimacy remain sources of contention. Furthermore, while it is fairly clear that trust in fairness is a precondition for citizens to confer legitimacy on an authority, the boundaries between different types of fairness are also contestable. (Arguably procedural justice theory has paid far too little attention to distributive fairness given how widespread across countries and cultures tensions are between the police and marginalised minority groups.) Does procedural justice imply distributive fairness? And does procedural fairness necessarily underwrite outcome fairness? Furthermore, the role of other preconditions for an authority to acquire legitimacy has been somewhat marginalised in procedural justice research – notably, the level of competence displayed by the authority in doing its job.

In my view, these are issues about the fine-tuning of the procedural justice perspective, rather than fundamental flaws in the approach. Any account of the processes by which people do (or do not) comply with social norms almost by definition needs to consider the role of fairness as a basic and universal human expectation. Procedural justice perspectives would appear to be of central importance in sustaining relations between the police and the policed – and especially in repairing relations between the police and the public when these have become seriously fractured. Nevertheless, it is important to recognise that procedural justice tactics may not necessarily help to guarantee legality and fair treatment against *objective* criteria of fairness. On the contrary, under some circumstances, when power-holders treat people politely, listen to them and explain the reasons for their actions, this may be construed as a form of manipulation. This is most obviously the case when social skills are deployed as a palliative or mask for substandard treatment, or to actually persuade people that unlawful actions are acceptable (cf Harkin, 2015; Meares et al, 2015). Critical legal theorists would extend this argument further to claim that systems of justice can serve to justify and perpetuate economic and social inequality (McBarnett, 1981; Norrie, 2001; Ramsay, 2006). These issues are explored in more detail in Chapter Six.

Conclusions

The evidence strongly suggests that procedural justice strategies are effective ways of securing people's compliance and cooperation within policing. As will be discussed in Chapter Five, there is a parallel body of evidence showing that the same principles apply in a wide range of other institutional and organisational settings. People value fairness, and fair treatment motivates people to cooperate with each other and comply with what others want of them. However, it is equally clear that treating people fairly is by no means the only way of getting them to do things. Instrumental strategies − offering inducements, rewards and punishments − can often work equally well. However, strategies of this sort require those seeking compliance to follow through and actually deliver the promised reward or threatened punishment. In the final analysis, both individuals and organisations have to make choices about the ways in which we get people to behave as we wish. Choices between normative and instrumental strategies are partly − and paradoxically − instrumental, involving judgement about the surest and most cost-effective route to achieving our goals. However, they are also unavoidably normative or ethical ones.

4

The policing of minority groups

This chapter explores the processes by which relations can break down between police and minority groups, especially those from visible ethnic minority groups. It presents evidence about the processes through which trust in the police can slip away if stereotyping and racial discrimination go unaddressed. The chapter devotes most attention to the policing of ethnic minority groups, in particular, to visible ethnic minority groups. However, the analysis is applicable to many other minority groups that are socially marginalised and exposed to routine discrimination. As in Chapter Three, we start with an extract from a qualitative study of policing (see Box 4.1). This extract illustrates the complexity of policing in settings where there is a long history of mistrust between the police and minority groups.

The policing of visible ethnic minority groups

Western industrialised democracies have a depressing track record in the policing of ethnic minority groups, in particular, visible ethnic minority groups. I use the term 'visible ethnic minority group' to be broadly equivalent to the various terms that are used in the UK to refer to 'non-white' groups, such as 'people of colour', 'black and minority ethnic' (BME) groups or 'black, Asian and minority ethnic' (BAME) groups. The reasons for using this terminology are twofold: first, I am drawing, in part, on international comparative research and UK terminology may not make sense for other countries; and, second, in understanding police treatment of different groups, ascription

Box 4.1 Trapped by history

23.50 The two officers I am with are called to assist two colleagues who are searching three young men. The officers have come across three young people smoking cannabis in a parked car. The car is in fact parked outside the home of one of the teenagers, who lives with his mother. Two of them are under 16, the third is 17. Two are black British; one is mixed race. When we arrive, the atmosphere is friendly, with the officers bantering quite happily with the three young men about cannabis and being a teenager. The three readily admit they have been smoking cannabis but say they don't have any left.

The officers explain to them that they have to search both them and the car. The three young men are quite happy for this to happen. One of the young men asks if his mother has to be made aware that he has been searched. The officer tells him he has no interest in telling his mother unless he has to arrest him. The three ask if they are going to be arrested, and the two officers tell them that they have no intention of arresting them, but suggest that they don't smoke their weed in a parked car at this time of night. One of the officers turns to the three young men and says there are only a couple of situations when three young men sit in a stationary car: the first is when they are up to no good, the second is when they are police officers looking for people who are up to no good. Since they didn't look like police officers, they must be up to no good.

At this point a woman leans out of one of the windows of the block of flats and starts shouting down to the three boys. The officers ask who the woman is and one of the boys replies, 'It's my mum.' The officer shouts up to the balcony that it is nothing to be concerned about and that they will be on their way very soon. The mother shouts down to let the officers know she is coming to join them. While she is on her way down the officer turns to the young boy and says that he may have to explain why he is searching him. The young man seems unconcerned. The woman comes out of the block of flats. She is very angry, pushes past her son and places herself about an inch from the officer. She shouts in his face, 'I have no respect for you whatsoever.' The officer replies: 'I'd like to be your son with that attitude. Can you leave as you're making matters worse?', to which she replies, 'I'm his mother, you can't tell me to go no fucking where.' The officer asks her to stop swearing. She refuses.

The three young men are quiet for a while, as are the four officers. The mother continues to shout at the officers for being 'fucking racist pigs', at which point the officers say to her that if she doesn't shut up and walk away, she'll be arrested. At this point her son starts to get angry and shouts at the officer, 'It's just bully-boy tactics, that's all you do, the problem with you is you have a problem with your height which is why you go about bullying black boys.' The officer replies: 'What I have a problem with is people who break the law – why are you starting to sound off? Until your mother showed up you were as good as gold.' The officers continue to search the car and the young men. Nothing is found. The mother continues to stand by the officers following them around the car; the officers ignore her. The checks come back from the control room and none of the three is wanted. The officers advise the three not to smoke weed in a stationary car and leave. The mother shouts after the officers that they are racists and should be ashamed of themselves picking on teenagers. The officers get in their car and drive off.

Source: May et al (2010: 44–45)

of an individual's ethnicity by the police and other organisations is more significant than that person's self-ascription – and the former is necessarily, in most cases, based largely on visual cues.

A starting point in understanding how the policing of minority groups goes wrong is to look at the migration history of minority and majority groups. Of course, taking a broad historical sweep, we are almost all descended from migrants. However, focusing on the last two hundred years, when recognisably modern police forces started to emerge, the majority groups in Europe were white, though with widespread migration into and within Europe of other white groups. The post-colonial era following the Second World War saw substantial migration to several European countries of visible minority groups, first from colonies and then from ex-colonies in the Global South.[1] The experience in North America is totally different: white migrants or their descendants – largely comprising emigrants from Europe – form the majority population, with indigenous groups, recent or more distant migrants from Latin America, and the descendants of black slavery forming significant visible minority groups. Australia and New Zealand similarly have majorities made up of white migrants or their descendants, with much smaller indigenous groups and a small but growing proportion of migrants from other Pacific countries.

At the risk of considerable oversimplification, it would seem that within developed European countries, most first-generation migrants, whether or not they are visible minority groups in their chosen country, arrived with positive attitudes towards the country and to its institutions, including the police. However, those migrants who would be regarded as visible minority groups in their new country were more at risk of discrimination, whether by the majority population or segments of it such as the police, teachers, employers and landlords. As a consequence, they were at greater risk than other migrants of experiencing social and economic disadvantage. Over time, therefore, the children, grandchildren and great-grandchildren of migrants from visible minority groups have been exposed to socio-economic factors that disadvantage a proportion of them, and render them at risk of greater contact with the police and, possibly, disproportionate involvement in some forms of crime.

Of course, this is not the only trajectory that the lives of migrants and their families can take. Many migrant families thrive, including those from visible minority groups, and they, and subsequent generations, become successfully integrated, both economically and socially. There may also be *some* migrants whose criminal careers started in their country of birth and continued in their new country.[2] Of course, there are also irregular migrants, some of whom have been trafficked and, in the process, find themselves locked into criminal networks. However, for the most part, migrants come to their new country by choice, with expectations of positive outcomes – which are by no means met in all cases. The relative advantages of the majority population, combined with hostile attitudes towards migrants, ensure that a proportion of migrant groups – and a large proportion of those from visible minority groups – suffer from processes of disadvantage.

The key mediating factors between material disadvantage and risk of contact with the police are factors such as having to live in neighbourhoods characterised by social disorganisation, in which young people are likely to be exposed to delinquent friends, and having limited access to high-achieving schools with low levels of delinquency, constraining the opportunities open to young people. To the extent that these processes affect families of migrants from visible ethnic minority groups, this will explain why successive generations of many migrant families from visible minority groups tend to acquire progressively more negative attitudes to their country and to its institutions. By contrast, migrants whose families are not members of visible minority groups – and whose migration history becomes 'invisible' over time – are much less likely to be subject to discrimination and disadvantage. A process of exposure to discrimination – whether by the police, teachers or employers – and to subsequent material disadvantage also offers an explanation for the over-representation of many visible ethnic groups among those passing through the justice system.

I should stress the general nature of the explanation that I am proposing. Behind the generalisation, there are, of course, some visible minority groups that experience a process of incorporation into their chosen country that leaves them materially no worse off in aggregate than the host community, and sometimes rather better off. I am also offering an explanation that is of particular relevance to European countries with colonial pasts, which have attracted generations of migrants from colonies and ex-colonies over the last six or seven decades.[3] Rather different explanations are needed to account for the experiences of both the descendants of black slavery and indigenous minority groups who have been displaced and marginalised in North America and the Antipodes. These groups have certainly been exposed to material disadvantage, though from a very different starting point. People migrating to European countries will have started a new life in their chosen country, and many, if not the majority, will have done so in a spirit of optimism – or at least that they were extending rather than curtailing their life opportunities. By contrast, the forced migration of largely African people to the New World as slaves, and the appropriation by white migrants of the lands of indigenous people, meant that both these groups were displaced and disadvantaged from the outset of the arrival of white settlers. Whatever the starting points of these different visible minority groups, the end result, in criminal justice terms, has been very significant over-representation in the courts and prisons – whether the reference point is the US, the UK, Australia, France or other European countries. The main reasons for this are to be found in the progressively worsening positions in society that successive generations of visible minority groups find themselves, consequent on patterns of discrimination at the hands of teachers, employers, the police and others.[4]

Attitudes to the police among migrant and visible minority groups: some evidence

This is not the place to attempt a comprehensive international review of the evidence about variations between groups in attitudes towards the police. There is a voluminous literature, especially in the US, and the overall picture to emerge is that visible minority groups tend to have less trust in the police, and rate their performance lower, than majority groups.[5] Here, I shall focus on the evidence of progressive deterioration across generations in relations between the police and visible minority groups from a positive starting point among those who actually migrated.

The Crime Survey for England and Wales (CSEW) provides good evidence about attitudes to the police among migrants relative to non-migrants. Bradford and colleagues analysed trust in the police among almost 29,000 people interviewed between 2008 and 2011, of whom approaching 4,000 were born outside the UK. Overall, migrants had *higher* levels of trust in the police than those born in the UK. The most recent migrants reported the highest levels of trust, which fell away as the period spent in the UK grew.[6] Those who had migrated as children reported lower levels of trust than other migrants, which were almost as low as rates of trust reported by UK-born respondents.

In Chapter Three, I discussed findings from the fifth European Social Survey, carried out in 2010. In further analysis of empirical legitimacy, Bradford and Jackson analysed the attitudes of almost 5,000 migrant respondents, comprising nearly 10 per cent of the overall sample.[7] Findings for the 27 countries covered by the analysis were broadly consistent with the picture on trust emerging from the CSEW. First-generation migrants generally conferred *more* legitimacy on the police than native-born respondents. Exceptions were those who had been in the country for five years or less – who did not differ from native-born people – and those who had arrived as children, who scored lower. Second-generation migrants tended to score the same or worse on legitimacy than native-born people. Other determinants of legitimacy such as levels of economic and social exclusion were important, and it is likely to be factors such as these that explain the orientation of second-generation migrants to the police. To simplify a complex set of findings, first-generation migrants generally give the police higher ratings of police legitimacy than native-born citizens, and second-generation migrants score the same as or worse than native-born citizens.

This analysis compared migrants to non-migrants, regardless of ethnicity. If one changes the focus from migrants to visible ethnic minority groups, a more pessimistic picture emerges. For example, the Metropolitan Police's Public Attitudes Survey shows that overall, including both migrants and British-born minority groups, African-Caribbeans, those of mixed race and Bangladeshis rate police legitimacy lower than white Londoners. Those from other minority groups either rate the police the same as white Londoners or – in the case of black Africans and those of Middle Eastern origin – higher. However, when migrants are removed from the analysis and the focus is on British-born minority groups, *all* visible minority groups rate the police lower than white Londoners, and these differences are all statistically significant with one exception, that is, people of Pakistani origin. The obvious conclusion to draw is that minority groups with lifetime experience of London policing draw on a deeper reservoir of negative experiences than white Londoners when making judgements about the police.[8]

Finally, the International Self-Report Delinquency study also can offer some international evidence showing similar patterns of attitudes to the police among teenagers. As discussed in Chapter

Three, we designed the third sweep of the survey to include measures of trust in the police and police legitimacy. We analysed findings according to migrant and visible ethnic minority status in six countries: England, France, Germany, the Netherlands, Scotland and the US. In all countries apart from Scotland and the US, both trust in the police and ratings of legitimacy among migrant teenagers was lower than native-born teenagers (in contrast to the aforementioned findings for adults). However, when account was taken of the social and economic differences between migrants and native-born teenagers, the differences disappeared. In other words, when comparing migrant and native teenagers with comparable socio-economic backgrounds, there was no difference between them.[9]

Disentangling the relationships between migrant status and visible minority status yielded some striking results. For all six countries combined, first-generation minority migrants (visible minority groups born abroad) rated police on trust and legitimacy the same as native-born white teenagers, controlling for demographic and neighbourhood factors. Second-generation minority migrants (visible minority groups born after their parents migrated) rated police slightly – but statistically significantly – worse than native-born teenagers. Native-born teenagers from visible minority groups rated the police even lower. Neither first- nor second-generation white migrants showed any difference to native-born white teenagers. In other words, we found the same pattern of progressive deterioration in ratings of the police as visible minority teenagers became distanced in time from the migration event that brought their family into the country. White teenagers with migrant backgrounds showed no such deterioration. The clear implication of these findings is that it is not migration status, but status as a visible ethnic minority, that is a significant determinant of teenagers' orientation to the police.

Escaping from hard power traps

Chapter Three of this book began with an extract from field notes of one of our studies that illustrated the dilemmas of policing when officers feel that the only policing style available to them is that of 'hard power'. It will be remembered that the encounter involved a search of a group of mixed-race young adults thought to be gang members. After the encounter, the officers told the researcher:

> We have to accept that we will never be in the right, or liked. We are damned if we do a lot of stop-and-searches, and damned if we don't. ... The local residents need to decide what they want, aggressive policing that keeps kids alive or 'nicey nicey policing' and more dead or injured kids. (May et al, 2010: 43)

It would be easy to dismiss this simply as a robust expression of the dominant front-line police culture: a tough-minded, cynical but well-intentioned outlook, with crime fighting and citizen protection as the central police mission. However, the possibility should not be dismissed out of hand that the police team under observation really had found themselves in a hard power trap. The officers thought that the only tactics that would have any immediate purchase on the problems they faced were ones involving coercion or the threat of coercive force – and to an extent, they may have been right. The basic command unit in question had such a long history of troubled relations between the police and the community that 'nicey nicey' procedural justice styles of policing would probably have been regarded as laughable, not only by front-line police, but also by those who they were policing.

However, in the same research project, police officers in another large city with an equally troubled history of tensions between the police and the local black community were seen to deploy precisely the sort of interpersonal skills in handling encounters that procedural justice theory advocates (largely as a result of local leadership by senior police managers). This raises the question how the police can reverse out of a hard power trap once they find themselves in one. One obvious point to make is that the police should take great care to avoid getting into that position in the first place – something of little comfort to those who find themselves in hard power traps constructed by the errors in policy and practice of their predecessors. Another obvious point is that repairing long-standing damage to relations between the police and the public is inevitably going to be a slow process.

How to negotiate out of a hard power trap is one of the hardest policing skills to acquire, and persuading the workforce of the importance of avoiding hard power traps is difficult. Moreover, building institutional knowledge on how to do so is equally difficult. However, the key tools required in the repair process are likely to be:

- clear leadership and advocacy of procedural fairness principles by chief officers and Basic Command Unit (BCU)[10] commanders;
- ensuring that internal styles of management are consistent with principles of organisational justice;
- training for front-line staff and their supervisors;
- equipping staff with more specific de-escalation skills[11] to do with the handling of conflict and defiance; and
- ensuring that effective community consultation mechanisms are in place.

We shall return to these issues in Chapter Five.

Conclusions

The policing of visible minority groups is one of the most contentious issues in criminal justice. These groups find themselves disproportionately ensnared in the justice systems of most, if not all, of those industrialised Western countries with ethnically diverse populations. Certainly, visible ethnic minority groups are over-represented in the prison populations of France,[12] Italy,[13] the Netherlands,[14] Spain, the UK[15] and the US.[16] This chapter has offered an explanation for these patterns that focused on the progressive social and economic marginalisation of migrants from visible minority groups over time, resulting from discriminatory treatment in systems of education, employment and justice. Leaving aside the unique history of migration and slavery in the US, European countries appear to have mismanaged the incorporation of minority groups over many generations.

Migrants have generally arrived in their new countries with optimism and positive attitudes towards the police and other institutions of their chosen country. The overall trend is that over time, and over generations, this positive outlook is overshadowed by negative experiences of the police, by falling trust in the police and by reductions in levels of legitimacy conferred on the police. The chapter ended with some pointers about ways of recovering relations between the police and some minority groups. Chapter Five considers in more detail some of the preconditions that are needed for achieving procedural justice styles of policing that may help repair fractured trust and rebuild legitimacy in these and other communities.

5

Embedding procedural justice in policing

This chapter considers some ways in which police leaders can best ensure that their workforces pay due attention to the legitimacy of their contacts with the public, and work harder at fostering their legitimacy in the eyes of the public. I suggested in Chapter Four that key factors in embedding procedural justice in police organisations are likely to be: clear leadership and advocacy of procedural fairness principles; adopting internal styles of management that are consistent with principles of organisational justice; training for front-line staff and their supervisors, including specific de-escalation skills in the handling of conflict and defiance; and ensuring that effective community consultation mechanisms are in place. This chapter focuses on issues of leadership and organisational justice, and discusses police training and qualifications. It does not cover community consultation in any detail.[1]

Leadership

At one level, embedding procedural justice principles in police organisations might seem to be simply a question of 'selling' the benefits to the workforce. To an outsider, these may seem overwhelming: treating people with procedural justice secures compliance and cooperation from those with whom the police have contact; it reduces non-compliance and thus increases officer safety; and it promises to save money, at least in the medium term, and thus increases the financial security of the organisation and its employees. There are also those more principled reasons for adopting procedural justice – that an indicator of a healthy nation is the degree to which those who exercise power over citizens behave fairly and with justice. As will be discussed in Chapter Six, the instrumental benefits – compliance, cooperation and safety – may secure immediate purchase with the workforce but there is a risk that focusing *solely* on these at the expense of arguments of principle could be counterproductive.

However, it would be a mistake to imagine that procedural justice will be an easy 'sell'. It is a truism that organisational change in *any* institution with a long history and traditions will demand a great deal of time and energy from leaders, who will also need to ensure that they carry their middle managers with them. There are reasons for thinking that this is especially true of change in policing. Many academics have described police occupational culture, with many common features. Robert Reiner (2000) identified seven defining characteristics: a sense of mission, suspicion (or cynicism), isolation/solidarity, conservatism, machismo, pragmatism and prejudice. The fact that similar accounts of police occupational culture, especially that of front-line staff, are found in many different countries and cultures suggests that shared structural features of police work are at play here: the stresses associated with the exercise of authority and coercive force; the risks arising from this, in terms both of resistance from those subject to coercive force and punishment for misconduct in the use of force; and pressures to deliver results.[2]

This occupational culture combines with the well-established observation that, of necessity, front-line police exercise more discretion than their superiors, which creates serious challenges for management. In response to these challenges – and perhaps also to maintain the public appearance of tight discipline and control – senior police managers in the past have adopted authoritarian management styles with paramilitary trappings, sometimes accompanied by cultures that tolerated the bullying of subordinates.[3] Whether such approaches to management were appropriate or effective in the past must be open to question. Whatever the case, both the traditional front-line occupational culture and the old-style authoritarian culture of senior managers are clearly incompatible with procedural justice styles of policing that accord dignity and respect to others, allow people voice, and explain the reasons for decisions. In Chapter Four, we discussed how these principles can easily be dismissed by front-line officers as unrealistic 'nicey nicey' policing.

Organisational justice as a prerequisite for procedural justice in policing

Part of the solution to these challenges facing police leaders is to ensure that the organisational ethos of their force is consistent with, and complementary to, principles of procedural justice. Research on organisational justice shares its origins with procedural justice theory. Initially, scholars such as Thibaut and Walker (1975) focused on the impact of fair processes in legal and policing contexts; however, by the 1980s, interest had broadened to examine fairness in other organisations.[4] Social psychologists have now been researching organisational justice in a range of settings for three decades or more but, until quite recently, have not explored the police or other organisations within the justice system – surprisingly, given the origins of organisational justice research and theory.[5] To summarise a complex field, organisational justice theorists aim to 'unpack' different facets of fairness in organisations and to trace the consequence for organisational performance of the presence or absence of fairness. The field has reached a consensus that a clear distinction can be made between *fair outcomes* in organisations (whether rewards and punishments are distributed fairly between individuals and groups) and *fair processes*. Some theorists simply equate the latter with *procedural fairness*, or *procedural justice*. Others make a distinction between fair processes (reflected in formal rules) and *interactional justice* (reflected in the personal styles of managers). Others disaggregate the latter into interpersonal and interactional justice. Table 5.1 depicts how the differing types of organisational justice can be summarised.

To some extent, how best to classify organisational justice is an academic argument. It is well established that the presence of *distributive justice* predicts rule compliance in an organisation, as well as satisfaction with pay. *Fair processes*, whether conceptualised

Table 5.1: The differing dimensions of organisational justice

Fair outcomes	Fair processes
Distributive justice (fairly allocated rewards and punishments)	Procedural justice (fair rules)
	Interactional justice (decent treatment)
	• interpersonal (respectful treatment)
	• informational (explaining, allowing 'voice')

and measured as one construct, two constructs or three, tend to predict a range of other behaviours valued by organisations:

- organisational commitment;
- trust in the organisation;
- perceptions of management legitimacy;
- job satisfaction;
- employee well-being;
- preparedness to work outside role ('going the extra mile'); and
- staff retention.

There is a growing body of evidence that principles of organisational justice are as applicable to policing as they are to other organisations, and that the benefits of workforce compliance, job satisfaction, well-being, health and staff retention flow from organisational fairness in policing no less than in other organisations. Staff surveys in the UK, Australia and elsewhere have found clear correlations between staff judgements about the fairness of their organisation and the expected benefits of fair treatment.[6]

This emerging body of research on organisational justice in policing has obvious and important – and yet too often ignored – implications for police leaders. The *relational* quality of management is as important, if not more important, than the sticks and carrots that managers can use to get results. If senior police officers wish to nudge their workforces in the direction of procedural justice, this is almost certainly achieved more effectively through active leadership than by re-engineering work processes or through training. The obvious way for senior managers to demonstrate a commitment to the fair and respectful treatment of the public is to ensure that these values are also applied within their organisation. In other words, achieving internal *organisational justice* may be a precondition for moving towards a *procedural justice* orientation in policing the public.

The research on organisational justice suggests that leaders who wish to implement *any* reforms effectively would do well to ensure that their workforce operates within an ethos of organisational justice. However, there are additional specific considerations when it comes to promoting procedural justice in policing: to exercise effective authority, police officers not only need to command legitimacy from those from whom they demand compliance, but also need to believe that they themselves are exercising legitimate authority.

Fostering self-legitimacy among front-line officers

Officers who do not feel confident in the legitimacy of their authority are unlikely to be skilful[7] in the use of this authority, and only first-rate actors can secure compliance from people when they feel that their entitlement to command is fraudulent. This sense of confidence in the legitimacy of one's own authority, or entitlement to authority, has been called *self-legitimacy* or *power-holder legitimacy* (in contrast to the *audience legitimacy* felt by those who are subject to police authority).[8]

The implications of emerging research on police self-legitimacy are clear. To ensure that their workforce adopts principles of procedural justice in their contact with the public, police leaders need to do everything they can to foster self-legitimacy among front-line staff. They need to know the circumstances under which power-holder legitimacy is likely to develop and thrive. Research shows that procedural fairness within the police organisation is a prerequisite for the development of self-legitimacy. This is hardly surprising. If every contact between the police and the public is a 'teachable moment' where people can learn something about the police, so too are contacts between rank-and-file officers and more senior staff. Any perceived unfairness or disrespect in these contacts serves as an endorsement by managers of these unwelcome qualities when front-line staff deal with the public.

The key message here is that getting the workforce to adopt procedural justice styles of policing involves rather more than putting in place a module of training on the topic at recruitment, supplemented by occasional top-up training. Those forces that still cling to traditional 'command-and-control' approaches to management need to embrace a thorough overhaul of organisational values and practices.

While police leaders obviously have a crucial role to play in setting the tone of their organisation and its values, middle managers and front-line supervisors both clearly also have a part to play in ensuring that their part of the police organisation observes principles of organisational justice. Without buy-in and, crucially, promotion by middle managers and supervisors, it is hard to envisage how *any* reform promoted by leaders will spread effectively through the organisation. However, sergeants and inspectors probably have a particularly important role to play in coaching and cajoling less experienced officers into developing a robust sense of self-legitimacy.

Training in procedural justice

Training programmes are an obvious – if problematic – point of intervention in organisational change, including training in procedural justice approaches. In-service training is a favoured solution because courses can be readily laid on. It is problematic because police working styles are, at least in part, a response to the nature of police work, and it is optimistic to expect that a short training course can reshape the ways in which police officers respond to the pressures placed on them. It is therefore surprising to find that research has quite a positive story to tell. Evaluations in the UK, US and Australia have shown that training in procedural justice can have durable benefits.

Wheller and colleagues (2013) mounted a randomised controlled trial involving the Greater Manchester Police. Unusually, the researchers were able to link survey data for victims with the officers who had dealt with their cases. They found that communications skills training based on procedural justice principles changed officer attitudes and behaviour, and had some impact on the ratings of officers by victims. They concluded that shifting officers' overall orientation was more important than teaching them communication tricks of the trade:

> Together these findings suggest that – rather than officers adopting specific techniques or skills they were taught on the course – training encouraged a general shift in the way officers approached interactions with the public. Officers in the treatment group potentially developed a greater awareness of the need to listen to, and build rapport with, victims of crime. (Wheller et al, 2013: 17)

Similarly, Skogan and colleagues (2015) found both short-term and longer-term changes attributable to procedural justice training in evaluations of a large-scale training programme mounted by the Chicago Police, involving almost 9,000 officers as well as civilian staff. However, the researchers cautioned their readers to have realistic expectations of what can be achieved in short training programmes, and argued that any effective change programme also needed to have refresher training, supervision by front-line managers (who also needed to be trained), the alignment of middle-management priorities with those of the force leadership, and attention to the overall ethos of the organisation.

A subsequent evaluation of the one-day Chicago programme followed up 8,500 officers, comparing officers who had been trained with others who were waiting for their training.[9] They found that training reduced complaints against the police by 10 per cent and reduced the use of force against the public by 6 per cent. Court settlements and compensation payments were also reduced. The two Chicago studies demonstrate that it is possible to change a style of policing that has been associated with popular distrust and the excessive use of force through training built around the concept of procedurally just policing.

Collectively, these three studies amount to strong evidence that officers can be trained to reframe their work through a procedural justice lens and modify the way they treat the public, in line with procedural justice principles, in ways that have a real impact on those they deal with. As discussed, training can only be one part of any police force's reform programme; however, the findings of these evaluations are striking precisely because the training 'dose' was fairly small. If even quite short courses can achieve measurable effects on officers' practice and on reactions from the public, the much more intensive degree-level education that police recruits will now experience in England and Wales could have a much more significant effect.

A policing degree: professionalisation and procedural justice

It may turn out that the 'professionalisation agenda' being pursued by police forces both in the UK and abroad may have very positive implications for those wanting to promote procedural justice. To some, professionalisation simply means delivering a better and more effective service; however, much more than this is involved for true professionalisation to occur. To understand what professionalisation really involves, it is worth taking a short detour into the history of the professional bodies that are responsible for the governance of occupations such as doctors and lawyers. These began to emerge in the 19th century as a means of regulating occupations requiring skill, judgement and integrity, involving geographically dispersed and autonomous generalist practitioners, where incompetence carries high social costs.[10] Their professional practice was – and still is – underpinned first by a body of technical knowledge, which the professionals have to acquire before they can practise, and second by a code of ethics, the breaching of which can lead to disbarment or disqualification. This mode of regulation is distinctively different from others, such as military hierarchy and administrative bureaucracies, which place more emphasis on authority structures. The burden of *knowledge* in these other, more hierarchical forms of accountability fall upon senior commanders or managers, with the requirements of *obedience* falling upon less skilled front-line staff.[11]

Historically, the police had clear quasi-military authority structures (even if, as discussed, front-line staff enjoyed extensive discretion). Recently, the police in England and Wales have moved rapidly towards professionalisation, with the establishment of a national 'warehouse' of research evidence,[12] the development of a code of ethics,[13] the establishment of a degree-level entry qualification[14] and the first steps towards a mandatory membership body. The rationale for this is that the increased complexity and diversity of policing requires front-line staff to exercise more autonomy and judgement than hitherto in handling incidents and crimes. In other words, staff are being expected to derive solutions to problems they encounter from the body of policing knowledge that they have acquired, rather than follow pre-specified procedures that they have been trained to follow. They will be less accountable to direct line management, and more guided by the evidence base and code of ethics.

The police professionalisation agenda is undoubtedly a contentious development. On the one hand, it promises significant improvements in the working life of police officers – in the shape of greater autonomy for front-line staff and a step further away from the old-style 'command-and-control' management style. On the other hand, it represents a threat to, and implicit criticism of, the competence of those officers with many years of experience but no degree-level qualification. Many of these will feel that the 'university of life' is a better preparation for the challenges of policing than formal education, and that degrees cannot guarantee some of the essential qualities needed for policing – emotional intelligence, compassion and common sense.[15] My own view is that requiring a degree-level entry qualification to join the police as a constable is a positive development. Recruits should have an opportunity to think hard about the role of the police in a complex and diverse society, and to be exposed to well-evidenced ideas about ways of securing commitment to the rule of law.

The degree-level entry qualification has clear implications for the take-up of procedural justice styles of policing. Procedural justice theory is fast becoming one of the key perspectives that inform academic thinking on the police, and it is hard to imagine a policing degree curriculum that did not give considerable space to this body of work. It remains to be seen to what extent the new system of degree qualifications helps to embed principles of procedural justice in police practice. At present, it is hard to judge how far down the road of professionalisation the UK police will travel. In England and Wales, there is a clear intention to transform policing into a knowledge-based profession to some considerable extent. To the extent that this is achieved, professionalisation will substantially advance the fortunes of procedural justice.

Conclusions

Embedding principles of procedural justice in British police forces amounts to a significant cultural shift, and police leaders who want to make this happen will need a multi-pronged change strategy. Visible and determined leadership, with strong support from middle managers, is clearly essential. One dimension to this is to convey to the workforce the real practical benefits that flow from the approach: cooperation and compliance from the public; greater officer safety; and fewer complaints from the public. Another important dimension is for leaders to ensure that the ethos within the force is consistent with principles of organisational justice. This is probably a precondition for persuading front-line staff that procedural fairness is expected of them in their dealings with the public. Organisational fairness is also closely correlated with officers' sense of self-legitimacy – or their confidence in wielding authority – which is another precondition for getting the workforce to adopt principles of procedural justice. Training has to be another strand in the change strategy, and the results of evaluations are positive. Finally, it seems possible that the way in which British policing is moving down the road to professionalisation may prove complementary to, and supportive of, procedural justice approaches to policing.

6

Ethics, justice and policing

This chapter[1] reflects on some of the ethical dilemmas that are raised by the approach to policing advocated in this book. As I have indicated in earlier chapters, there are some real ethical issues facing both front-line police officers concerned with maintaining their own authority and those more senior officers who need to foster the legitimacy of their organisation. At the level of both the individual officer and the institution, the ethical dilemmas spring from the use of what might be seen as 'low-visibility techniques of persuasion' for securing compliance and for getting people to acquiesce or accept police action that is not in their best interests. The chapter starts with a discussion of these low-visibility persuasive techniques. It then examines, in turn, the ethical dilemmas faced by individual officers and by the police as an institution.[2] In the final part of the chapter, I suggest a resolution to these ethical issues.

To anticipate my conclusions, a focus on fair and respectful treatment does indeed provide a set of behavioural techniques that *could* be deployed to secure public tolerance of illegal practices or compliance with illegitimate regimes (or with judicial systems, police forces or other forms of authority). However, in relation to individual officers' behaviour, any approach needs to specify where the boundaries fall between behaviour that is genuinely courteous and respectful, on the one hand, and that which is manipulative, on the other. (Put simply, policing styles must respect the boundaries between charm and deviousness.) More important, however, police organisations need to recognise that building trust in the police and fostering police legitimacy is not simply a tactic for securing compliance, but actually reflects values that ought to underpin democratic policing. Policing styles should be built firmly on a foundation of social rights, with a recognition that treating people with fairness and dignity flows naturally from the adoption of social rights principles.[3] The chapter argues that policing (and the criminal law) has – and should have – an unavoidable connection to morality, while recognising potential risks in proposing close connections between moral standards and the enforcement of the law.

Low-visibility techniques of persuasion and police legitimacy

There is a family of approaches to governance variously labelled as techniques that are 'low visibility', 'non-intrusive', 'persuasive' and 'nudges'. According to one leading commentator, 'What makes [persuasion] a distinct mode of governance is that it targets not the incentive structure, but people's beliefs about the social world, thereby modifying their understanding of what represents their (personal and/or collective) best interests' (Mols et al, 2015: 81).

This set of approaches for securing compliance is distinct from strategies that *directly* adjust the balance of costs and benefits that attach to any given course of action. In securing compliance with the criminal law, the state has traditionally applied strategies that are designed almost entirely to increase the costs of non-compliance – through strategies of deterrence. Techniques of persuasion leave the costs and benefits of non-compliance unchanged but adjust the 'choice architecture' (to borrow a term from behavioural economics) that people encounter in calculating these costs and benefits.

Social marketing approaches

While strategies of deterrence have been the dominant way in which states secure compliance from their citizens, there has in parallel been a long tradition of harnessing the concepts and techniques of marketing to social policy, and to *persuade* rather than *incentivise* citizens to behave in particular ways. Governments – and interest groups – have been applying advertising and marketing methods since the start of the 20th century, if not before, especially during the two world wars.[4] Social marketing approaches can appeal to self-interest, or can apply various forms of normative leverage, in order to persuade people to conform. These latter approaches are usually called *social norms approaches*. They may appeal to the need to conform to perceived norms (descriptive norms) or to moral principles (injunctive norms). An advertising campaign that simply relayed statistics about high levels of compliance with any given regulation would be appealing to descriptive norms, while one that drew attention to the social harms associated with a particular behaviour would rely for their impact on injunctive norms. Simply alerting people to descriptive norms can be effective, presumably because most people are more comfortable with conformity than non-conformity. More often, however, advertising may exploit the existence of injunctive norms. This can be highly effective in getting across messages on a range of social issues, a good example being a very long-running series of UK advertisements to reduce young people's levels of drunk driving by stressing the potential harm caused to others, rather than the risks the driver runs of punishment.

Nudges

Nudge theory can be regarded as a 'close relative' of social norms marketing approaches, adopting some of their tenets and assumptions, and adding others. 'Nudging' the public has become part of the repertoire of social policy implementation in the US, the UK, Australia and elsewhere. For example, the UK government set up a special unit, the Behavioural Insights Team (BIT),[5] to develop nudge techniques in order to persuade people to adopt healthy behaviour, 'green' behaviour, charitable giving and compliance with a range of regulations. It now operates in several other countries. A nudge is any aspect of the choice architecture that alters people's behaviour in a predictable way, without forbidding any options or significantly changing their economic incentives.[6] There are many examples of nudges, some of which are clearly in the social marketing tradition described in the previous section, whilst others emerge more directly from behavioural economics[7]. Examples of successful nudges include: changing the default position, for example, in establishing opt-out rather than opt-in procedures for healthcare or organ donation; encouraging people to comply with tax requirements by telling them that the vast majority of people pay their taxes; and sending people personalised reminders when demanding payment of vehicle tax, including a personalised image of the car in question, showing its number plate.

Procedural justice strategies in policing

Securing normative compliance – the approach advocated in this book – can be seen in broad terms as a member of this family of persuasive techniques. It involves securing compliance not by increasing the probability of punishment, but by conveying to citizens that the criminal law, and its agents, wield authority that is legitimate and thus is *worthy of compliance*. As such, it is a non-instrumental approach that operates at a *normative* level by creating or reinforcing a sense of moral obligation to obey the law. Arguably, these strategies meet the definition of a 'nudge' – although, to date, I have not seen anyone else make this connection. Civil and polite treatment by the police certainly leaves unchanged the economic or instrumental incentives to comply with (or ignore) their instructions – and civility is cheap, and easy for recipients to discount, even if they cannot actually avoid it.

Ethical issues for low-visibility approaches to compliance

Libertarians (whether left libertarians or libertarian conservatives) tend to bridle at strategies that invisibly or non-intrusively regulate behaviour. Preferring the clarity of instrumental or coercive strategies, which fully confer agency on citizens in choosing between compliance and non-compliance, they see non-instrumental approaches as patronising, diminishing or infantilising of citizens. These approaches share, potentially, a number of ethical dilemmas:

- reducing the autonomy of citizens as decision-makers by *covertly* reframing their decisions about legal compliance;
- potentially requiring or encouraging *insincerity* on the part of those exercising authority; and
- *misleading* citizens about the motives of power-holders.

Non-instrumental approaches, in particular, nudges, have been widely and enthusiastically adopted; however, they have also been criticised for being manipulative, a violation of human autonomy and an 'elitist choice-limiting technique' (Mols et al, 2015: 87), as well as for overextending the reach of government into everyday decision-making. Thaler and Sunstein (2008) clearly anticipated this and branded their nudges as a form of 'libertarian paternalism' from the outset. They argued that a nudge must not deny people the option of making the 'wrong' choice, and the wrong choice must be easy to make. Advocates would argue that nudges simply alter the choice architecture available to people in order to stack the odds slightly more in favour of the desired decision.

There is nothing especially new about these concerns about the erosion by government of citizens' agency. The dystopian novels of Aldous Huxley (*Brave New World* [Huxley, 1932]) and George Orwell (*1984* [Orwell, 1949]) dealt with the risks of psychological manipulation in autocracies. However, the urgency of their warnings appears to have been lost with the passage of time and repetition – and perhaps also as the techniques that Huxley and Orwell railed against have become so incorporated into everyday life as to become commonplace. Here, I do not propose to examine *in general* the ethical and political issues that attach to persuasion and nudgery – except to suggest that despite some risks, low-visibility measures can provide sensible, practical and cheap solutions to problems of compliance. Rather, my focus is narrow, being specific to the ethical issues that arise from procedural justice approaches – and their resolution. I wish to suggest that the ethical and political concerns about non-instrumental approaches to behaviour management can also apply to procedural justice strategies and, in so doing, take particular forms. Analysis of these strategies can be provided either at the level of individual practitioner, in which case the issues that arise are clearly ethical ones, or at the institutional or societal level, in which case the issues become political and cultural ones.

Ethical issues at an individual level

There are genuine issues to do with sincerity and honesty when police officers and other legal authorities deploy procedural justice tactics to secure compliance, though these should not be overstated. It is a commonplace in discussions of the craft of policing that demeanour is central to managing difficult situations. The idea is laughable that officers should avoid using their social skills to nudge fractious citizens into compliance. However, there is a boundary between behaviour that is civil and courteous, and that which is manipulative. I will not attempt to outline where this boundary falls, but it clearly falls *somewhere*, with gross insincerity and deception falling the wrong side of the line.

There are related issues to do with what supervisors can reasonably demand of their staff. Any employer can require their staff to treat people with courtesy and respect – which involves the *performance* of particular social skills – but it is more problematic to expect staff to *feel* respect for those they are serving. Employers may want their staff to internalise a set of values that will guide the treatment given to people but it is unclear in the policing context whether this should simply be a hope or aspiration, or a firm expectation for which employees may be held accountable through a code of ethics, and ultimately a condition of employment.[8]

The key to resolving these issues is to clarify the motives that underlie procedural justice tactics. If the tactics are seen, first and foremost, as instruments for securing compliance, then it is likely that the ethical issues surrounding insincerity and deception will rapidly emerge. However, if the *primary* justification for the tactics is that they are supported by a set of ethical standards in enforcement, then this helps to resolve the ethical dilemmas relating to instrumental justifications for procedural justice tactics as it should ensure that the pursuit of compliance does not displace the values that underpin procedural justice tactics. We shall return to this at the end of the chapter.

To date, a focus on legitimacy and on procedural fairness has been promoted in the UK in a rather instrumental way, with advocates tending to prioritise what is in it for the police, rather than what is in it for the policed. Although there is quite persuasive evidence that these benefits are real (as discussed in Chapter Three), further research should establish whether there has been any overselling of the 'ends' of procedural justice in terms of crime reduction. However, there seems little doubt that one motivation for emphasising the extent to which procedural justice secures deference, cooperation and compliance was that this was, and probably still is, considered to be one of the best ways to 'sell' the idea to otherwise sceptical police officers. This create an obvious hostage to fortune: if it turns out that the links between perceptions and experiences of the police and future law-related behaviours are weaker than commonly assumed, does this mean that the police do not need to worry about behaving in a fair way? Equally, and relatedly, it also risks undermining ethical take-up of the core idea by reducing it to the level of cost–benefit calculus.

Ethico-political issues at an institutional and societal level

Procedural justice researchers in the US have already examined the risks that procedural justice strategies could be used to legitimate styles of control that are illegal, unethical or undesirable. To use the terminology discussed in Chapter Two, legal authorities may exploit their empirical legitimacy (in the eyes of the policed) to justify or render acceptable forms of behaviour that lack normative legitimacy (or legitimacy assessed against agreed objective norms). The obvious example is the undue restriction of liberty through stop-and-search (or stop-and-frisk in the US), made palatable by the style in which searches are executed. It is also possible – if not probable – that in heterogeneous societies, the majority of the public may easily be led to support the overbearing treatment of minority groups, so long as they themselves are treated relatively well by police. Marxist theory and the tradition of legal realism offer recognisably similar arguments, though ones that are framed at the societal level. The Marxist version of the argument is that a particular narrative about legal institutions can provide an 'ideological cloak' that hides the existence of the material inequalities of capitalism from both the beneficiaries and the victims of the system. Thus, the principle of equality before the law guarantees at a formal level – but not at a substantive one – the equal treatment of the rich and poor, or the weak and powerful. The argument is that this appearance disguises the – less than fair – economic or material conditions of capitalism. The argument is basically one about 'false consciousness', on the same lines as Marx's much-quoted phrase that religion is the opium of the masses,[9] whereby forms of ideology serve to secure popular acceptance of – or at least resignation to – social arrangements that are less than fair.

The tradition of legal realism, or critical legal theory, is associated with similar arguments, without necessarily being aligned closely with the Marxist perspective of historical materialism. The basic orientation of legal realism is that judicial outcomes are necessarily shaped by factors outside of the formal law – whether these are the values of the judiciary or the broader world view of social elites or other powerful interest groups. Whatever these external factors might be, the way in which they operate to serve particular interests may be cloaked by ideological narratives about equality before the law and about the impartiality and fairness of officers of the law.

Of course, the importance of securing consent to the rule of law was recognised from the start of Anglo-American policing. The nine Peelian principles that Rowan and Mayne set out in 1829 in their *Instructions* for the Metropolitan Police in London could be inserted almost without change into a modern procedural justice training manual.[10] Take the fifth principle, for example:

> 5. To seek and preserve public favour, not by pandering to public opinion, but by constantly demonstrating absolutely impartial service to law, in complete independence of policy, and without regard to the justice or injustice of the substance of individual laws, by ready offering of individual service

and friendship to all members of the public without regard to their wealth or social standing, by ready exercise of courtesy and friendly good humour, and by ready offering of individual sacrifice in protecting and preserving life.

One can only guess about the extent to which the architects of the new police consciously recognised that they were in the business of appearance management (or ideology construction). The Metropolitan Police Act 1829 was introduced against a background of economic crisis and frequent riots. The threat posed by the 'dangerous classes' and the fear of revolution were ever-present for the ruling elite in the first half of the 19th century. It would be surprising indeed if it never occurred to Peel and his two commissioners that a civilian, civil, respectful and impartial police offered a better chance of securing public order than naked force.

As mentioned earlier, empirical research has demonstrated that at an individual level, procedural justice tactics can render extra-legal police behaviour tolerable to the public. People will accept police practices that are extra-legal provided that they see these practices as fair, and they do not expect officers to be punished for such behaviour (Meares et al, 2015). Clearly, this represents an undesirable outcome for procedural justice theorists. It is harder to evaluate claims that at a societal level, the police, or the institutions of justice more broadly, can provide an ideological cloak to protect unfair social structures from challenge. These arguments lie close to the boundary between empirically testable propositions and sociological interpretation. Much of the sociological writing on the topic is clearly interpretive, offering a cogent narrative rather than verifiable evidence. However, political psychologists have more recently offered some empirical support by demonstrating that the demographic correlates of 'status quo bias' are consistent with system justification theory (for a review, see Jost et al, 2010).

For our purposes, it is enough to accept the *possibility* that styles of authority can serve as an ideological cloak that masks the true nature of the social and economic arrangements of the day. It is perfectly conceivable that the way in which the 'modern police' were introduced in the 19th century formed part of the ideological apparatus that tamed the dangerous classes. It is equally plausible that in some modern-day jurisdictions, authorities use procedural justice approaches to shield illegal or unfair practices from challenge. The more important question to ask is how these risks, whether at the individual or societal level, can be effectively mitigated.

Also relevant may be that the unit of analysis in procedural justice research has tended to be individual people (which is hardly surprising given the psychological roots of the theory). It is possible that this has inhibited researchers from considering the institutional level, in particular, the potentially problematic interaction between the ways in which individual police officers treat people on a one-to-one basis and the ways in which particular groups or communities are policed by the organisation as a whole. For example, a force could embrace procedural justice in uniformed policing – not least as a claim to their own legitimacy – yet authorise unethical covert surveillance and undercover operations (they may even do the former to offset the latter). The same citizens could find themselves on the receiving end of both modes of policing, with quite predictable outcomes. This problem is sometimes made explicit in critiques of public order policing, where police liaison officers work in what is effectively a procedural justice mode in order to build links with protestors or football fans, yet also work alongside forward intelligence and evidence-gathering teams who use other tactics. The work of the liaison officers is intended to offset the tensions arising from enforcement activity, yet, in reality, both liaison and evidence-gathering work can feed directly into aggressive or oppressive modes of policing.

Resolving the ethical dilemmas of procedural justice

Consistent themes have run through this discussion of the ethical and political dilemmas raised by procedural justice approaches. Procedural justice approaches raise in a particular form the ethical and political problems that are generally created by low-visibility non-instrumental approaches to social control.

The strategies and tactics of procedural justice may be used – or misused – as a means to ends that are inconsistent with principles that accord respect and fair treatment to citizens. For procedural justice approaches to be done successfully in this way, power-holders need to disguise the ends that they are actually pursuing.

It is fairly clear what should be done to mitigate the risks posed by individual officers who use procedural justice tactics in ways that are clearly manipulative. Training and professional development need not only to equip officers with the social skills needed to deploy procedural justice tactics effectively, but also to ensure that they appreciate that there is a boundary between courteous sincerity and manipulation that should not be crossed. Probably the most persuasive way of getting this message across to the workforce is to show that the costs of insincerity, once identified, are high: people are sensitive to attempts at manipulation, which can often evoke a hostile reaction. This is, of course, an instrumental argument that appeals to officers' self-interest, along the same lines as the argument that procedural justice tactics make officers safer. It is a fine judgement whether this approach amounts to getting people to do the right things for the wrong reason. There is obviously a place for pragmatism of this sort – this is a preferable outcome by comparison with people doing the *wrong* thing for the wrong reason. However, it is probably better – though harder – to ensure that instrumental justifications of this sort are accompanied by normative ones that make the connections between procedural justice tactics and underlying principles about good policing.

There are two main responses to the criticisms that at an institution or societal level, procedural justice strategies serve as an ideological cloak that masks social injustice and seduce citizens into consent.[11] The first is to recognise that the institutions of justice *can* function in this way, but that when they do, the remedies do not lie within criminal justice. The second, and more ambitious, response is to try to ensure that the institutions of justice are built upon principles of democracy and human or social rights that are consistent with social justice. Such institutions would appear better placed to inculcate in their members a sense that treating those they serve with openness, dignity and respect is the right thing, in and of itself, to do (Bradford and Quinton, 2014). However, the counterargument of critics would be that this is merely to reinforce the fabric of the ideological cloak. The principles of justice institutions and their members may count for little if the wider system they serve is marked by inequity.

Making convincing connections between procedural justice approaches and underlying principles would need to appeal to conceptions of citizenship that privilege autonomy and agency, and that make some reference to human rights, or social rights. In other words, it would involve recognition of the fact that procedural justice theory may provide a powerful descriptive account of the processes that secure compliance with authority but cannot by itself form a prescriptive theory about good policing. We shall return to the issue of the values that can underpin procedural justice styles of policing in the final chapter.

Conclusions

This chapter has explored some of the ethical and political issues that are raised by procedural justice approaches to policing. Both in individual contacts between the police and the public, and at a societal level, problems can result from the use of low-visibility techniques for securing compliance. At an individual level, it could be argued that the 'choice architecture' of compliance with the law is being redesigned without people being aware of this, and that their autonomy as citizens is being eroded, when police officers manage them into compliance through a display of civility and respect. At a societal level, the appearance of the police as an even-handed and fair institution that 'plays by the rules' may serve as a sort of 'ideological cloak' that hides structural inequality and unfairness from public view. I have suggested that the risks of these problems are real if and when the police pursue the instrumental benefits of procedural justice – compliance, cooperation and officer safety – without any significant commitment to the ethico-political foundation of procedural justice. The primary justification for procedural justice approaches to policing is not that they are effective approaches for securing compliance with the law and commitment to the rule of law – though these are obvious benefits – but that those exercising coercive state power have a duty to treat citizens fairly and with respect.

7

Closing thoughts

This book started with a summary of its key themes, and I would trespass on readers' patience if I offered yet another summary by way of conclusions. However, there are some issues that I have ruminated upon without reaching any firm or satisfactory conclusions – and this may be a sensible place to rehearse them. First, there is the question I raised, though did not really answer, in Chapter Two about the extent to which a good police officer is a *morally* good one. Second, there are questions relating to the risks of coupling policing and the law too closely to *public morality*. Finally, I still feel a residual sense of unease about the possibility that police will see procedural justice principles simply as a set of tactics for securing compliance with the law, and will construe the perspective simply as a series of behavioural tricks – or social skills – which need to be acquired to deliver effective policing. The best way of mitigating this risk, I suggest, is to render explicit the normative or ethical foundations underpinning procedural justice approaches.

Competence, ethics and morality

In Chapter Two, I sketched out the beginnings of a definition of good policing, suggesting that it involves striking the best possible balance between coercive and consensual policing. I recognised that good policing necessarily involves the use of coercive force in some situations, but argued that officers should strive to minimise its use. A central criterion in assessing the quality of policing should always be whether it enhances or reduces police legitimacy. By implication, competent police officers should adhere to principles of procedural justice in the way in which they treat those whom they police. Thus, a good police officer is someone who treats the people with whom they have contact fairly and respectfully, accords them dignity, listens to what they have to say, and explains the reasons for their decisions.

The question that I posed at the end of Chapter Two was whether good police officers simply have to *perform* fairness and respect, or whether they are required to hold and internalise the values that underpin legitimate policing. To find some answers to this question, it may be helpful to consider what expectations we have of those in a range of other forms of work. For some occupations, all we expect of practitioners is a level of technical competence, with civility being a non-essential bonus. Skilled trades, for example, plumbers and electricians, usually specify standards of practice narrowly and contractually – if indeed they are articulated at all – although these may be backed by industry bodies' codes of practice and legislation about standards. In contrast the 'mature' professions, such as law and medicine, have well-developed codes of ethics, including references to the values that practitioners are expected to hold. For example, the General Medical Council's ethical guidance to medical practitioners requires them to show respect for human life, to be honest and open, and to act with integrity.[1] There is a clear expectation that practitioners should have the best interests of their client at heart, and not simply fulfil explicitly or implicitly the contract into which the client has entered. Indeed, it is for this reason that doctors and lawyers have *clients* and skilled tradesmen have *customers*. (Of course, many of those who have contact with the police are customers only in an ironic sense.)

Where on this spectrum of professional obligations does policing fall? Historically, rank-and-file officers have been expected to simply do their job with basic competence: obey the orders of their supervisors; follow rules and regulations; and conform to recognised best practice. However, alongside this rather minimalist account of what is expected of front-line police, there has always been a variety of richer narratives that portray various moral dimensions to police work. Both in film and television dramas and in the sociology of the police, one can find accounts of officers working as 'philosopher, guide and friend'.[2] As a counterpoint to this, there are also accounts of the police as 'crime-fighting crusader' – hard-bitten, with the cynicism of experience and the pursuit of ends through whatever means are available, but still with a serious commitment to crime fighting.[3] While resulting in very different styles of policing, these characterisations have in common a sort of vocational commitment that involves altruism and a sense of service.

As the police service moves towards professionalisation, the extent to which police leaders should foreground these issues of vocation and altruism will become a matter of choice. A key question is whether officers should be recruited and promoted against criteria of *character* or of *competence*. Character includes the quality of moral decision-making and judgement, while competence includes ethical behaviour. The distinction between acting morally and behaving ethically is a fine but important one. Ethical behaviour does not necessarily flow from moral decisions: one can do the right (ethical) thing for the wrong (less than moral) reasons, or do the wrong thing for morally respectable reasons. Concealment of motivation and misjudgement about ability to bring about intended consequences are both commonplace.

I tend towards the position that the police service should demand ethical *behaviour* from its workforce but should stop short of requiring individuals to hold particular *values*, or to adopt particular moral standpoints or forms of moral reasoning. There are two reasons. First, behaviour is public but values and moral reasoning are private. Inferring someone's motivation from their behaviour is fraught with possibilities of error. Second, developing a professional identity, including a coherent set of moral values, is a long-term process that needs experience and, arguably, organisational support. Police evolve into good police officers.

The College of Policing has struck a sensible balance between issues of ethics and those of morality in its code of ethics.[4] In common with the British Medical Association's (BMA's) code, this is framed almost entirely in terms of the behaviour that is expected of members, though it makes oblique reference to moral standards. Like the BMA code, it points to values that are expected of members but does not go into any detail, and does not explore the implications of these requirements. For example, it requires officers to abide by principles of respect in all their dealings with people but does not explore whether they should *feel* respect or simply *perform* respect. This ambiguity is probably constructive.

Law, policing and morality

Legal scholars and reformers have long debated the proper scope of the criminal law, and the limits that should be set to its reach.[5] The central core of the criminal law is concerned with the punishment of behaviour that harms other people, but at its penumbra, it forbids behaviour that most people regard as immoral without necessarily inflicting harm on others. Examples include attempting suicide (a criminal offence until 1961), blasphemy (decriminalised in England and Wales in 2008), homosexual behaviour between consenting adults (criminalised until 1967), incest between males and females (but not same-sex incest) and the use of various psychotropic drugs.

Viewed over the very long term, the criminal law in most European countries emerged from the religious regulation of moral norms. There has been an evolution from the enforcement of religious (or moral) norms to a narrower function restricted to the preservation of individual rights (including the right to be protected from harm). Thus, in most states, the criminal law has progressively shed laws related to offences such as blasphemy, sacrilege and homosexuality. The argument that the limits of the criminal law should be defined by reference to the preservation of individual liberty and freedom from harm has – largely – been won.[6] The most famous debate on this topic, at least in common law countries, was that between Herbert Hart and Lord Devlin in the run-up to the legalisation of homosexuality in the 1960s. This debate prompted extensive academic analysis of the relationship between law and morality, and the limits of the criminal law.[7] Hart was a member of the Committee on Homosexual Offences and Prostitution, which led to the Wolfenden Report, recommending that homosexual behaviour should be decriminalised.

Hart's argument – reflected in the Wolfenden Report – was that homosexual behaviour between consenting adults involved no public harm – or no breach of rights – and that the law thus had no right to try to regulate that behaviour. He also argued that criminalising behaviour that was regarded by the majority as immoral would lead to the oppression of minorities and impose an unjustifiable brake on changes in social mores. The Wolfenden Report expressed this perspective neatly: 'There must remain a realm of private morality and immorality which is, in brief and crude terms, not the law's business.' Devlin responded to the Wolfenden Report in his 1959 British Maccabean lecture entitled *The Enforcement of Morals*, arguing that the state is entitled to legislate in matters of morality and that the criminal law should be shaped by public morality.[8] He argued that some degree of correspondence between public morality and the criminal law was essential in ensuring the legitimacy of the justice system, and that legislators who retreated from this position were jeopardising the system's legitimacy. On the particular issue, Hart clearly held the winning cards, and homosexual acts between consenting adults were legalised in 1966. It is clear that the logic of Hart's argument could also point to the legalisation or at least decriminalisation of other criminalised behaviour that harms nobody beyond the perpetrators, and the principle that harm to others is the principal justification for criminalising behaviour is now central to penology.

Does procedural justice theory represent a challenge to the principle that private morality has no place in the criminal law – and the policing of it? In narrow intellectual terms, the answer must be 'no'. Procedural justice theory can assert the interdependence of law and morality without undermining the boundaries between public behaviour and private morality. The obvious argument to deploy is that the close coupling of moral rules and legal rules should only apply when both sets of rules involve clear harm to others, and thus an intrusion into their freedom. In other words, the criminal law can be regarded as providing underpinning support only for those moral rules that protect people's rights to be free from harms inflicted by others.

However, in broader political terms, I can see risks in some police responses to the – very clear – evidence that 'moral alignment' between the public and their police is a central element of police legitimacy in the eyes of the policed. Procedural justice theory proposes that the sense of moral alignment – the sense that the police are 'on our side' and 'share our values' – flows from polite, respectful and fair treatment. However, this approach could drift into a sort of shared moralism, whereby the private morality (or supposed immorality) of minority groups is regarded by both the police and the moral majority as an appropriate focus for policing. It remains to be seen how significant a risk this becomes; however, it is worth mentioning that some penologists have proposed that the sentencing of offenders should be aligned with public preferences if the legitimacy of the courts is to be preserved.[9] This form of 'intuitive justice' privileges majority public opinion in a way that could threaten liberal 'Enlightenment' values – something that has clear parallels with these risks.

The coronavirus pandemic, discussed in the Postscript to this book, raises somewhat similar issues about the tensions between the legal obligations placed on citizens and the civic duties to which they are subject, especially in times of emergency. The legal obligations during 'lockdown' were defined more narrowly than the government instructions or requests made to the public and, initially at least, some police forces set out to police the latter as well as the former. The police service rapidly adopted a more tenable position: that their job was to enforce the legislation and not the more far-reaching instructions of the government.

Procedural justice, human and social rights, and democratic values

Chapter Six considered in some detail the ethical risks associated with the use of procedural justice styles of policing to build police legitimacy. I argued that the fundamental justification for procedural justice in policing was normative: that treating people fairly and respectfully, according them dignity, and giving them voice are the *right* things to do, not simply a tactic for securing compliance. In other words, the instrumental benefits in pursuing procedural justice – compliance, public cooperation, officer safety and workforce well-being – may be significant but they do not provide an adequate and enduring justification for adopting procedural justice principles. I suggested that a commitment to social rights provided the normative underpinning for procedural justice principles. Without such a foundation, procedural justice would increasingly be seen by the public simply as a set of behavioural tricks – and appropriately devalued and dismissed as such.

One obvious framework to provide a normative foundation for procedural justice approaches is that of human rights. This is the route followed by Andrew Coyle (2009) in his book *A Human Rights Approach to Prison Management*. Table 7.1 sets out the various international instruments that he cites in support of this.

Coyle was writing in the context of prison management but it is worth noting that almost all these instruments refer not specifically to prison inmates, but to people subject to detention or deprived of their liberty. In other words, they are equally

Table 7.1: What the international instruments say

International Covenant on Civil and Political Rights, Article 10:

All persons deprived of their liberty shall be treated with humanity and with respect for the inherent dignity of the human person.

Basic Principles for the Treatment of Prisoners, Principle 1:

All prisoners shall be treated with the respect due to their inherent dignity and value as human beings.

Body of Principles for the Protection of All Persons under Any Form of Detention or Imprisonment, Principle 1:

All persons under any form of detention or imprisonment shall be treated in a humane manner and with respect for the inherent dignity of the human person.

The African Charter on Human and Peoples' Rights, Article 5:

Every individual shall have the right to the respect of the dignity inherent in a human being and to the recognition of his legal status.

American Convention on Human Rights, Article 5 (2):

All persons deprived of their liberty shall be treated with respect for the inherent dignity of the human person.

Source: Coyle (2009)

applicable to anyone who is arrested by the police – and they all refer to the need to treat people with dignity or respect.

It might be argued that a human rights framework of this sort is too narrow to be applied to procedural justice principles. Some would argue that to have any purchase of the behaviour of nation states, human rights have to be fundamental, specific, justiciable and enforceable. It may be that the expectation that one will be treated by state officials with dignity and respect is better conceptualised as a social right. Thus, the Charter of Fundamental Rights of the European Union sets out a much broader – and looser – set of social rights than the European Convention on Human Rights. The first article of this charter states that 'Human dignity is inviolable. It must be respected and protected.' Thus, it privileges one of the core principles of the procedural justice approach. I will leave it to others to argue whether the expectation of decent treatment from state officials is a human right, a social right or simply a democratic right. However, there is no doubt in my mind that a good state will recognise an obligation to treat its citizens with respect and dignity, with equality of treatment, and with integrity. As Nagin and Telep (2017: 56) put it: 'As a matter of principle, citizens are deserving of fair treatment by the police and other authority figures within the CJS [criminal justice system] irrespective of whether that treatment fosters compliance with the law.'

It remains to be seen whether reform-minded police forces make the connections between procedural justice and social rights. This may not be the most auspicious time to do so. There are signs of a shift in political mood in many industrialised democracies, with a move away from Enlightenment values, towards national self-interest and insularity, scepticism about human and social rights, hostility towards the independence of the judiciary, a rejection of so-called 'political correctness', and scepticism about technical expertise and scientific knowledge.[10] It is too early to say if the UK is firmly set to join other countries in embracing these right-wing authoritarian values but the government is committed to reviewing both the UK legislative framework for human rights and the judiciary's role in reviewing government interpretations of legislation. (The UK incorporates the European Convention on Human Rights into the Human

Rights Act 1998.) Moreover, from 2021, assuming that Brexit follows projected timelines, the Charter of Fundamental Rights of the European Union will no longer apply in the UK. It would be very sad indeed if current enthusiasm within UK policing for procedural justice was affected by this change of political mood, so that the service lost sight of the essential normative foundations underpinning the approach.

Postscript: Policing the COVID-19 pandemic

The COVID-19 pandemic emerged as this book was being finalised. Countries throughout the world introduced regulations restricting freedom of movement, designed to slow down the spread of infection. These regulations were intrusive for most people, curtailing much of their normal activities, and securing public consent to comply with them involved difficult decisions for both legislators and the police. This postscript was written six weeks after the number of COVID-19 cases peaked in the UK, as restrictions began to be eased. It provides an account of the policing of the pandemic in the UK, focusing on the ways in which the regulations challenged the legitimacy of both the police and politicians. I have assumed that the cautious lifting of restrictions will continue and that the rate of infection will continue to slow as we return to normal life– or at least a new form of normal life. This may involve a process of intermittent surges in cases followed by the temporary reimposition of restrictions. My focus has been on the months of March, April and May 2020, covering the period from when the UK government recognised the gravity of the threat posed by the pandemic to the first easing of the 'lockdown' restrictions in mid-May.

The context

The first documented case of COVID-19 was thought, at the time of writing, to be in Wuhan, China, and the first patient's symptoms began on 1 December 2019. By the end of December, Chinese doctors were beginning to realise that a pneumonia-type epidemic was under way. In early January, there were signs of the virus spreading to other countries. The Wuhan lockdown began on 22 January, and at the end of January, the World Health Organisation declared a public health emergency of international concern. Cases were emerging throughout the world, including in the US and mainland Europe, with the UK confirming its first case on 31 January.

Controls with varying degrees of stringency were put in place internationally throughout February. Tighter lockdown measures restricting people to their homes were introduced in many countries in early/mid-March, including Italy, France and Spain. In the UK, the prime minister announced on 6 March that the main requirement on the public was to wash their hands to the tune of 'happy birthday' for 20 seconds.[1] There was press speculation that this more relaxed approach than that of other European countries was informed by a strategy that involved building up 'herd immunity' in the population. However, shortly after that, results of new modelling presented to politicians on 14 March showed that without more intensive measures, this approach would involve an unacceptably larger number of deaths than had been previously estimated.[2] Preventive measures then became increasingly more stringent in the UK, culminating in the announcement of lockdown arrangements on 23 March, which required most people to stay at home for most of the time.

Under lockdown, most shops were shut, as were pubs, clubs and other places of entertainment. Apart from essential workers, the working population worked from home, where this was possible, or stopped work. Most air and rail travel stopped. More than 6 million of those whose jobs were suspended joined a government job-retention scheme, where 'furloughed' employees received 80 per cent of their monthly salaries up to a maximum of £2,500, and a further half a million self-employed people joined a parallel scheme. However, an unknown number of people slipped through this support net and had to apply for the pre-existing – and less generous – system of unemployment benefits. Schools and universities were closed.

At the time of writing, daily numbers of confirmed diagnosis of COVID-19 were in decline, as were numbers of COVID-19-related deaths. However, the fall was less dramatic than those in mainland Europe, where lockdown measures had been introduced two or three weeks earlier. The number of cases worldwide was estimated at almost 6 million in late May, with 350,000 deaths. In the UK, the number of cases was estimated at 270,000, with 38,000 deaths directly attributed to COVID-19 and deaths that were directly or indirectly caused by COVID-19 put at 60,000.[3] Whether there would be a second wave of the pandemic was unclear, though medical professionals were warning of the possibility.[4]

The regulations

The regulations were enabled through the Coronavirus Act 2020, which was introduced to Parliament on 19 March, passed on 23 March and received Royal Assent on 25 March. The Act was time-limited and gave wide discretionary powers to the government, including the restriction or closure of public gatherings and public transport, the closure of businesses, and the detention of people suspected of infection. It also included a range of powers to respond to the economic challenges posed by the pandemic. The Act was supported by a series of statutory instruments (SIs)[5] for the different countries in the UK, the key one for England being the Health Protection (Coronavirus, Restrictions) (England) Regulations 2020 (SI 350).[6] Sections 6 and 7 set out the restrictions that created the lockdown, which were to last for the duration of the emergency period or until amended.

Section 6 stipulated that nobody could leave their home without reasonable excuse. The main reasonable excuses were specified as the need to:

- obtain food and medicines and other necessary supplies for the household, their pets and vulnerable people, supplies for the essential upkeep, maintenance and functioning of the household;

- take exercise either alone or with other members of their household;
- seek medical attention;
- provide care or help to a vulnerable person, or to provide emergency assistance;
- travel for the purposes of work (including voluntary work), when this couldn't be done from home; and
- attend a funeral of a household or family member.

Section 7 specified that during the emergency period, no person may participate in a gathering in a public place of more than two people unless these are all members of the same household or are doing essential work.

The powers available to the police to enforce these requirements are set out in Section 8. These include:

- directing that person to return to their home or taking them there, using reasonable force if necessary;
- directing people to take their children (or children in their care) home, and to ensure that their children observe the restrictions; and
- direct prohibited gatherings to disperse, and to direct people in the gathering to go home.

Anyone in breach of the regulations has committed a criminal offence and is liable to be punished with a fine or fixed penalty notice. At the time of writing, around 15,000 fines had been issued in England and Wales. The Act and the SIs specify that all enforcement activity should be reasonable and proportionate. The first relaxation of these regulations came on 13 May, when SI 500 extended the list of reasons for being away from home.[7] Key changes were to permit people to leave their homes for open-air recreation, not simply exercise, and to permit households to meet with one other person outside at any one time.

A significant factor is that government advice on lockdown behaviour was more extensive in scope than the regulations themselves. Thus, the advice that people should always keep a two-metre distance between themselves and anyone who is not in their household was *not* covered by the English regulations.

Nor was there originally any legal basis for restricting exercise to one period per day, for a maximum of an hour. Thus, a distinction can be made between government *guidance, advice* and *requests* relating to the lockdown and the *legal requirements* whose breaches can be prosecuted.[8]

Impact of the regulations

The lockdown was clearly effective in reducing the number of COVID-19 cases, though less dramatically (at the time of writing) than in mainland Europe. The daily number of COVID-19-related deaths had also fallen. Thus, the lockdown appeared to be achieving its primary objective.

Overall, the lockdown regulations commanded wide public support, especially at the outset. Clearly, there was some flouting of the regulations. A Nuffield-funded UCL survey covering several time points throughout the lockdown found that there was a reasonable level of compliance with the regulations through the initial lockdown, with young people less compliant than their elders. Around two thirds of people reported complete compliance, with signs of a gradual decline over the lockdown period.[9] It seems likely that compliance with the regulations will weaken over time, though this will probably depend on the government's skills in conveying the right messages – which, as we shall discuss later, has sometimes been weak.

The regulations have clearly had very different effects for different social groups. For those in well-paid salaried occupations with work that can be done at home, the income losses have been minimal. The same is largely true for those in receipt of pensions. At the same time, the opportunities for discretionary spending have shrunk dramatically – in shops, restaurants, cinemas and theatres, and on holidays and outings. Many in these groups will probably emerge from the COVID-19 emergency no worse off, and possibly better off. However, for many other groups, the pandemic will have been financially disastrous. Those in less well-paid service industries – which usually depend on the discretionary spending of the affluent – will have suffered even if they have been furloughed, and the growing number of unemployed will face greater hardship.[10]

The regulations have had some striking, if unintended, consequences for policing. The lockdown has substantially altered the opportunity structures for crime. During full lockdown, most shops have been shut and supermarkets shoppers have been subject to close supervision by staff, queuing for entry and often subject to elaborate routing systems, reducing opportunities for shoplifting. House burglary is very much riskier as most houses have been left empty only for short periods. Similarly, cars are more closely supervised by owners, and rarely left in autocrime hotspots such as large car parks. Motoring offences have fallen simply because very many fewer cars were on the road. Crimes committed in public space, notably, robbery and theft from the person, are riskier because potential offenders are much more visible to the police. According to the National Police Chiefs Council, police forces have seen crime reduce by 28 per cent in the four weeks to 12 April compared to the same period last year. However, the falls have been offset to some extent by rises in domestic violence and by other crimes that occur within households.

The legitimacy of police enforcement of the lockdown

Given the speed with which the lockdown restrictions were designed, were put into law and came into effect, it is hardly surprising that the initial police response was variable. Some forces opted for initial high-visibility action, including roadblocks, for example, in Devon and Cornwall, and the use of drones to deliver warnings about the regulations, for example, by Derbyshire Constabulary. It can be assumed that the intention, at least in part, behind these headline-grabbing tactics was to signal to the public that the regulations were being enforced. There were some clear variations in levels of enforcement, as reflected by the number of fines issued. For the period from 27 March to 11 May, there were high levels of fine enforcement in London (906), the Thames Valley (866) and Devon and Cornwall (799), and low levels in Warwickshire (31), Staffordshire (52), Kent (117) and Cambridgeshire (120).[11] These variations are only partly explained by variations in the populations served by these forces.

There is, of course, no requirement for forces to adopt identical strategies for policing an emergency of this sort, especially when each force had to get its approach in place at speed. Perhaps of more concern are that the same statistics indicate that people from minority ethnic groups were 54 per cent more likely than white people to attract fines. At this point, one can only speculate as to the reasons; however, the analysis I offered in Chapter Four of relations between the police and minority groups is obviously relevant.

Initially, there was criticism of police overreach in enforcing the regulations, most noticeably by a recently retired Law Lord and member of the Supreme Court, Jonathan Sumption, in an interview given to the BBC World at One programme on 30 March.[12] His criticism, which attracted widespread press attention, made two main points. The first was that the restrictions imposed at the end of March were a hysterical overreaction driven by public concern:

> So yes this [pandemic] is serious and yes it's understandable that people cry out to the government. But the real question is: is this serious enough to warrant putting most of our population into house imprisonment, wrecking our economy for an indefinite period, destroying businesses that honest and hardworking people have taken years to build up, saddling future generations with debt, depression, stress, heart attacks, suicides and unbelievable distress inflicted on millions of people who are not especially vulnerable and will suffer only mild symptoms or none at all, like the Health Secretary and the Prime Minister.

With the benefit of hindsight, this may seem very overstated given the limited length of time for which there was a tight lockdown and the severity of the pandemic's impact in the UK. There are around 600,000 deaths in the UK annually, and COVID-19 led – directly or indirectly – to 60,000 extra deaths over the average for nine weeks in the months of March, April and May. Judging by the lockdowns in France and Italy, it seems likely that an early and more restrictive lockdown in the UK might have avoided many of these premature deaths.

However, Lord Sumption made an additional point that carries far more force:

> In some parts of the country, the police have been trying to stop people from doing things like travelling to take exercise in the open country, which are not contrary to the regulations, simply because ministers have said that they would prefer us not to. The police have no power to enforce ministers' preferences, but only legal regulations – which don't go anything like as far as the government's guidance.

It is an important point that the police should aim to secure compliance only with rules and regulations that have the force of law. To expect the police to interpret and enforce government instructions, requests and guidance that lack statutory backing risks creating a large deficit in their legitimacy; it would involve the police acting as an arm of the government, without legal cover, which Lord Sumption characterised in his interview as a step towards a police state. It is unclear whether the gap between the regulations set out in statutory instruments and the guidance issued by the government was intentional. The architects of the lockdown may have followed the well-tried negotiating strategy of demanding more than you really expect to get in relation to their instructions; alternatively, it may have proven too legally complex to capture the spirit of the instructions fully in legislation. Whatever the case, in hindsight, it would have been better to ensure that government instructions were much more closely aligned with the regulations.

Even the regulations themselves are inevitably loose, the key ones in Section 6 of the SI relying on a requirement to stay as home unless one has a 'reasonable excuse' for going out. The list of examples is broad but not exhaustive, and clearly open to interpretation – as emerged in the case of Dominic Cummings (discussed later). Deciding whether someone offered a reasonable excuse would inevitably involve the police in highly discretionary decision-making, with risks of pushback and challenges from those whose excuses were rejected.

The very muddy landscape of enforcement practice at the start of the lockdown was clarified a great deal by guidance to police forces from the National Police Chiefs Council and the College of Policing. The summary version as it was in May 2020 is reproduced in Figure 8.1 (College of Policing, 2020). This helpfully directs officers to enforce only the regulations, not the government's instructions, advice and guidance. It is also very clear that officers should respond in a graduated way, starting with engagement and explanation, moving if necessary to encouragement and persuasion, and using enforcement powers only as a last resort. The Crown Prosecution Service also issued guidance on 26 March, update on 13 May to reflect the loosening of the lockdown.[13]

Trust in government pandemic policy

The legitimacy of police enforcement of the COVID-19 regulations is tightly tied up with public trust in government policy in relation to the pandemic. If the police story is one of improving trust after a shaky start, trust in government policy followed a different trajectory.

The government entered the pandemic emergency with some strengths and some weaknesses. They had won a convincing majority of 80 seats in the December general election, giving them a clear mandate to 'get Brexit done'. On the other hand, many people thought that the election had been lost by Labour rather than won by the Conservatives, and the country remained deeply polarised over Brexit. Added to this, the prime minister had acquired a reputation, deservedly or not, for dishonesty, a limited grasp of detail and a lack of seriousness as a senior politician. On the basis of press coverage, the early response by the government to the emergency was regarded as weak, failing to reflect both the real severity of the crisis and the urgent need for action.

However, the shift in approach in mid-March triggered by the new estimates of the number of deaths that could occur in the absence of a lockdown seemed to carry public support. Surveys indicated that the public mood about COVID-19 was

Figure 8.1: National Police Chiefs Council and the College of Policing: 'Policing the pandemic: the Act, the Regulations and guidance'

Source: College of Policing, 2020

risk-averse,[14] and Boris Johnson's approval ratings were probably helped by his hospitalisation and treatment in intensive care in April, following a positive diagnosis of COVID-19 at the end of March. As the government began to ease the lockdown restrictions from 10 May onward, public support dipped.[15]

Four factors have probably been at play. First, while senior politicians claimed that the government's policy was 'following the science', there was a great deal of reluctance to make the scientific advice publicly available. For a time, the government even refused to publish the membership of the Scientific Advisory Group for Emergencies (SAGE) and its various subgroups. This probably damaged public trust in the claims that policy was evidence-driven. Second, the government mismanaged several procurement processes – for protective equipment for medical staff, for ventilators, for testing equipment and, most recently, for an effective contact-tracing system. Ambitious targets were regularly announced and then missed. This persistent pattern of failure will have dented public trust in government competence.

Third, the announcement of the relaxation of lockdown restrictions was handled in a way that led to both public confusion and ridicule. In a speech on 10 May – in advance of publication of more detailed plans – Johnson announced that the lockdown's slogan of 'stay at home' was to be replaced by 'stay alert', and that people should show 'good solid British common sense' in following the revised and loosened regulations. People were unsure about precisely what they should be alert about, but it was clear that this style of messaging signalled that staying at home was no longer a priority, and that people could exercise their discretion in interpreting the loosened regulations. Various ministers offered their own – sometimes conflicting – interpretations of what the loosening in the restrictions actually meant. It is hard to judge the extent to which the ambiguities and nuances in the announcement were planned or accidental.

Finally, various prominent public figures attracted media attention by breaking the lockdown regulations that they were associated with. Dr Catherine Calderwood, Scotland's Chief Medical Officer, resigned on 6 April after being discovered breaking the regulations by visiting her second home.[16] A month later, Professor Neil Ferguson, whose work prompted the lockdown, resigned from his position on SAGE after it emerged that he broke the regulations by meeting a lover in his home.[17] By themselves, neither of these events will have greatly damaged trust in government policy as neither people were politicians and both immediately apologised and resigned. However, the handling of possible breaches of the regulations by Dominic Cummings, senior adviser to the prime minister, caused outrage. When his wife began to show symptoms of COVID-19, he did not self-isolate with her in his London home, but drove with her and their child 260 miles to his parents in Durham and self-isolated there. Whether this constituted a breach of the regulations is contested, and both Cummings and Johnson argued that exceptional circumstances justified the trip: the argument was that Cummings's young son was potentially very vulnerable, with both his parents sickening with COVID-19. Durham Police subsequently said that they did not regard this as a breach of Section 6 of the regulations, though they emphasised that they were making a judgement about a likely breach of the regulations, not government advice. However, they judged that he had probably broken the regulations by visiting a beauty spot by car after his recovery, and that if any police officer had encountered him on this trip, he would probably have been told to return home.[18]

The fallout from this was clearly serious for the government. The story emerged on 23 May and dominated the media headlines over the bank holiday and for days thereafter. Cummings and Johnson repeatedly denied that there had been any breach of the regulations, arguing that there was sufficient discretion built into the rules to permit deviation from them in exceptional circumstances. There was no sign of any public apology.[19] This caused considerable outrage, with intense criticism not only from opposition politicians, but also from conservative backbenchers, religious figures, scientific advisors, senior police and National Health Service (NHS) staff. It was a textbook example of how to squander public trust. By the end of the month, around 100 conservative MPs had been openly critical of Johnson and Cummings. Surveys conducted by the Oxford Reuters Institute found that trust in government and trust in politicians showed very large falls between April and May.[20]

This episode coincided with announcements of further relaxations of the lockdown restrictions, with some shops opening at the start of June and the remainder opening two weeks later. Small groups of friends could gather in parks and gardens. The messaging from the government – intentional or not – was clearly that adherence to the regulations was now a matter of personal judgement. Both the Cummings incident and the news about loosened restriction had broken over a hot and sunny bank holiday weekend, and people took to the beaches in very large numbers, with limited scope for effective social distancing. It felt like the lockdown had come to an end.

Notes

Chapter 1

[1] See Elias (1997 [1939]) and Pinker (2011, 2018).

[2] See especially Eisner (2003, 2014).

[3] The most accessible summary is to be found in Kahneman's (2011) book *Thinking, Fast and Slow.*

[4] While most forms of crime fell from the mid-1990s until the end of the first decade of the 21st century and now appear to be plateauing, there is growing evidence of increasing levels of violence associated with drug dealing and gangs, and an increase in Class A drug use, especially cocaine. For a recent review, see Hales et al (2020).

[5] Deterrence theory assumes that people are generally responsive to threats of punishment in the event that they ignore a law, or a rule or request. Deterrence theory usually distinguishes between the certainty of punishment, the celerity of punishment (or the speed with which punishment follows lawbreaking) and the severity of punishment. Precisely how responsive people are to the certainty, celerity and severity of punishment remains hotly contested, even if most people subscribe to theories of deterrence to some extent.

[6] At the time of writing, the government was proposing to ensure that for crimes attracting long sentences, release should not occur until two thirds of the nominal sentence has been served. It was unclear whether the aim was simply to reduce the gap between the nominal sentence and time served, or to increase sentence length by a third.

[7] Sir Kenneth Newman published in 1985 a now largely forgotten booklet *The Principles of Policing and Guidance for Professional Behaviour* (Newman, 1985), which was an intelligent development of the Peelian principles of policing. The argument was that preserving consent to the rule of law – by securing the Queen's peace – should take precedence over securing compliance with the letter of the law. It had the tentative support of Leon Brittan, the then Home Secretary, and strong misgivings among some 'law and order' blowhards.

[8] Behavioural economics theorists Richard Thaler and Daniel Kahneman both poke intelligent fun at the idea of the 'Econ', their shorthand for the conception of rational calculators proposed by traditional economists (see Thaler and Sunstein, 2008; Kahneman, 2011).

⁹   For a full discussion, see Part 1 of Robert Reiner's (2010) *The Politics of the Police.*

¹⁰ These are to be found in Bittner (1974: 30, 35; see also Bittner, 1970).

¹¹ For a fuller discussion of these themes, see Loader and Sparks (2013). They present a subtle account of 'the inseparable connection between empirical discovery and normative judgement that the concept of legitimacy carries with it'.

¹² See Ayres and Braithwaite (1992) and several chapters in Drahos (2017), including ones by John Braithwaite (2017), Valerie Braithwaite (2017) and Kristina Murphy (2017).

Chapter 2

¹ President Obama commissioned this report in the wake of several highly contentious shootings by police of black suspects, including that of Michael Brown in Ferguson, Missouri (see President's Task Force, 2015: 1).

² See the Patten Report (1999).

³ For definitions and an extended discussion, see Roberts et al (2003). For a more recent discussion of penal populism in England and Wales, see Jacobson and Hough (2018).

⁴ Most senior politicians make sure that they do not leave any evidence about their populist intentions. However, Tony Blair was wrong-footed by a leaked memo in July 2000, where he identified a need to respond to 'gut British instinct'. He saw a need to 'think now of an initiative, for example, locking up street muggers. Something tough, with immediate bite which sends a message through the system.' The memo suggests that the then government was obsessed with the message rather than the substance of policy. For more details and a fuller discussion of penal politics at that time in the UK, see Allen and Hough (2008).

⁵ See: www.gov.uk/government/speeches/police-reform-theresa-mays-speech-to-the-national-policing-conference

⁶ See: www.gov.uk/government/speeches/home-secretary-at-the-apcc-and-npcc-partnership-summit

⁷ Among academics, Robert Reiner has considered legitimacy in some depth, for example, in successive editions of *The Politics of the Police* (Reiner, 2000, 2010), as has Ian Loader (for example, Loader and Mulcahy, 2003; Loader and Sparks, 2013). Sir Robert Mark's programme to tackle corruption in the Metropolitan Police is notable, as were Lord Scarman's (1981) report into the Brixton Riot and Lord Macpherson's (1999) report into the murder of Stephen Lawrence.

⁸ There were only 13 references to 'police legitimacy' in Britain's leading criminological journal – *The British Journal of Criminology* – in the second half of the 20th century, compared with 77 in the 20 years since 2000 – a 12-fold increase of references per year. Notably, Her Majesty's Inspectorate of Constabularies, Fire and Rescue Services (HMICFRS) conducts police effectiveness, efficiency and legitimacy (PEEL) programme inspections of police forces annually. For a fuller discussion of the development of

legitimacy studies and work on procedural justice theory, see Bradford (2020).

[9] For a fuller discussion, see Hinsch (2008, 2010). He uses the two terms 'normative' and 'empirical' legitimacy in contrast to 'objective' and 'subjective' legitimacy, and I have followed his lead. However, both pairs of terms have currency and deciding which pair to use is a matter of personal preference.

[10] A phenomenon widely reported by the media in Bangladesh and India, for example.

[11] A constant theme in police and detective dramas is that of the crusading cop or private investigator who pursues noble ends through questionable means. The 1971 film *Dirty Harry* is still one of the best known in this genre (for a discussion, see Klockars, 1980).

[12] For a fuller conceptual and empirical justification of this position, see Jackson et al (2015) and Jackson (2018).

[13] Some scholars, such as Tankebe (2013) and Sun et al (2018), have regarded the obligation to obey not as a constituent element of the concept of legitimacy, but as a consequence of it – on the basis that the sense of obligation can be either normative or prudential. For an empirically based counterargument, see Posch et al (2020).

[14] Most developmental psychologists suggest that children acquire concepts of fairness between the ages of four and eight (for example, Blake et al, 2015). Evolutionary biologists (for example, Fehr et al, 2008) would argue that an understanding of fairness is 'hard-wired' into our brains, reflecting the survival value of preparedness to cooperate.

[15] Of course, stories for children can be nuanced and include portrayals of corrupt authority and moral lawbreaking, with Robin Hood being the obvious example.

[16] See especially the report of the Scarman Inquiry into the Brixton riots (Scarman, 1981).

[17] See, for example, Bottoms and Tankebe (2012), Tankebe (2013) and Sun et al (2018).

[18] See IPCC (2015). For an extended journalistic account, see *The Guardian* (2017). See also Home Affairs Select Committee (2018).

[19] It remains unclear whether some minority ethnic groups, notably, people of African-Caribbean and African origin, are disproportionately involved in the criminal justice system because of over-policing, or because they are over-represented in socio-economic groups that are at risk of offending – or because of an interplay between these factors (cf Bowling and Phillips, 2002; Lammy, 2017; Phillips and Bowling, 2017). Some evidence is presented in Chapter Three.

[20] For example, Saunders (2010).

[21] See, especially, Messner and Rosenfeld (2001, 2010).

[22] Recent empirical support in the UK can be found in the series of studies by Farrall and colleagues on the impact of Thatcherite economic policies on crime trends in the 1980s and 1990s (for example, Farrall and Hay, 2014;

Farrall et al, 2017). However, the centrality of socio-economic factors as primary crime drivers has been questioned, especially in view of the crime drop occurring at the end of the 20th century in many countries (see, for example, Van Dijk, 2013).

23   See, for example, Messner (2015).

24   In reality, British colonial policing tended to deploy coercive force through paramilitary styles of policing and though 'penal excess'. It has been argued that the differences between domestic and colonial policing have been overstated, and that there are plenty of signs of 'hard policing' in aspects of domestic policing (see Bell, 2013). Reiner (2010) has suggested that the Peelian ideal of consensual domestic policing was as much myth as reality – the myth being constructed to defuse hostility to the introduction of the 'modern' police.

25   The term 'soft power' was coined by the US political scientist Joseph Nye (1990).

26   The 'Soft Power 30' index has been built and maintained by the US consultancy Portland (see: https://softpower30.com).

27   The main one being that in their professional role, politicians *are* rational calculators, for whom normative pressures are only marginally effective.

28   Sherman's (1993) 'defiance theory' is an intuitively attractive complement to legitimacy theorists' accounts of legal compliance.

29   Muir's (1977) classic analysis of policing refers to this as having 'a tragic sense', in which the good police officer grasps the nature of human suffering.

Chapter 3

1   The evidence to support the procedural justice perspective is substantial. Key sources include Mazerolle et al (2013), Sunshine and Tyler (2003), Tyler (2003, 2006, 2011a, 2011b), Tyler and Fagan (2008), Tyler et al (2010, 2015), Schulhofer et al (2011), Papachristos et al (2012), Huq et al (2011a, 2011b) and Tyler and Jackson (2014).

2   See May et al (2010) and Hough (2013).

3   In the 2010 ESS, 26 countries collected usable data for the module on trust and legitimacy that we designed.

4   See Jackson et al (2011a, 2011b, 2012) and Hough et al (2013). The analysis presented here is on 26 countries, with a total sample of 52,000 adults, plus the results from the Japanese survey.

5   See Enzmann et al (2018) and Roché and Hough (2018).

6   See Tsushima and Hamai (2015).

7   For the international review, see Jackson (2018). Bradford et al (2014b) report on the South African findings, and Jackson et al (2014) report on the survey in Lahore, Pakistan.

8   See Jackson et al (2020).

9   See Farren and Hough (2018b). Mediation analysis was carried out to assess what proportion of the predictive power of trust on preparedness to offend could be attributed to perceptions of legitimacy. However, in the

countries where trust has no predictive effect, we cannot say whether this reflects real cultural differences or data problems.

[10] See Murray et al (2020). ISRD has city-based samples. In England, samples of schools were drawn from Birmingham and Sheffield. In Scotland, samples were drawn from Edinburgh and Glasgow. The Scottish police had greatly increased the use of stop-and-search from around 2005 to 2015, when our fieldwork took place. Thereafter, the use of the tactic was significantly curbed.

[11] See Skogan (2006). Our ISRD3 analysis also found support for the 'asymmetry thesis' in the context of police contacts with teenagers (Farren et al, 2018: 185). However, Oliveira and colleagues (forthcoming) have suggested that the thesis may have been overstated.

[12] See, for example, Nagin and Telep (2017).

[13] A replication of this study in Scotland failed to secure similar findings, possibly because the traffic police there already followed principles of procedural fairness and the police pushed back against what they regarded as inappropriate attempts to tell them how to do their job (Bradford et al, 2015).

[14] This is an explanation that appeals to particular forms of legal socialisation. For fuller discussions, see Tyler and Trinkner (2017) and Bradford (2020). See also Bradford et al, (2014a).

[15] For an extensive review of legal socialisation, see Tyler and Trinkner (2017).

[16] The origins of social identity theory are usually associated with the social psychologists Henri Tajfel and John Turner (1979, 1986).

[17] Analysis by Bradford (2014) is relevant here. He examined a sample of young black and minority ethnic (BME) Londoners, divided into those who reported a sense of belonging to a non-UK country (as well as a sense of belonging in the UK) and those who felt a sense of belonging only to the UK. He found that 'police behaviour appeared more identity relevant for people who felt they were citizens of a non-UK country, while for those who identified only as British there was a weaker link between procedural fairness and social identity'.

[18] For an intelligent discussion of 'vouching' and 'clinching' evidence for social policy making, see Cartwright and Hardie (2012).

[19] See, for example, Harkin (2015) and Radburn and Stott (2019).

[20] See Bottoms (2002), Kahneman (2011) and Wikström et al (2012).

Chapter 4

[1] Notably, to France, Belgium, the Netherlands, Portugal and the UK. In Germany, the *gastarbeiter* (or guest worker) programme in the 1960s led to a significant Turkish population.

[2] However, there are competing explanations and perspectives on the factors that draw some groups into crime. For a discussion, see Phillips (2019).

[3] There is, of course, a longer history of migration of visible minority groups into European countries from the 16th century onwards, much but not all of it associated with the slave trade.

[4]   This is not to rule out entirely explanations that appeal to cultural differences between some visible minority groups and the majority group in their chosen country. There are two main sorts of argument put forward: one is that some migrant groups import values from their home country that are criminogenic; the other is that organised crime groups actually import illegal immigrants to work under the direction of gangmasters to engage in shoplifting, robbery, burglary or drug distribution. However, for most groups, the balance between economic and cultural pressures is tipped heavily in favour of the former – despite media and popular stereotypes.

[5]   For a thorough review of relations between the police and ethnic minority groups in the US, see Weitzer and Tuch (2006).

[6]   See Bradford et al (2017). Interpretation is complicated by the fact that those who had migrated to the UK at least 40 years ago reported higher levels of trust than those who had been in the country between 20 and 40 years. The authors suggest that this might reflect the particularly turbulent state of police–migrant relations when the latter group arrived.

[7]   See Bradford and Jackson (2018).

[8]   See Bradford (2014).

[9]   See Farren et al (2018) and Murray et al (2020).

[10]   BCUs are typically led by chief superintendents in England and Wales. Previously known as divisions, and typically covering populations from 50,000 to 200,000, they are now much more variable in size and have various labels. In England and Wales, there are around 230 BCUs. In London, the basic policing unit is the borough.

[11]   For a discussion of de-escalation techniques, see Quattlebaum et al (2018).

[12]   France does not collect statistics on ethnic status, but for an interview with Didier Fassin, see: www.cairn.info/revue-mouvements-2016-4-page-19.htm?contenu=article#

[13]   For a report that discusses both Italy and Spain, see: http://eujusticia.net/images/uploads/pdf/Justicia_Network_Disparities_in_Criminal_Justice_Comparative_Report_2018-1.pdf

[14]   See: www.tandfonline.com/doi/full/10.1080/10282580.2018.1415049

[15]   For the UK, see: https://assets.publishing.service.gov.uk/government/uploads/system/uploads/attachment_data/file/639261/bame-disproportionality-in-the-cjs.pdf

[16]   For the US, see: www.naacp.org/criminal-justice-fact-sheet/

Chapter 5

[1]   For an excellent US practitioner guide, including issues of community consultation, see Quattlebaum et al (2018).

[2]   For a fuller discussion, see Reiner (2016). Reiner's analysis of the structural factors shaping occupational culture draws on Skolnick's (1966) classic book *Justice Without Trial*.

[3]   In a study of chief officer misconduct that we carried out for the College of Policing (Hales et al, 2015; Hough et al, 2016), interviewees described bullying as a feature of an increasingly outdated authoritarian

'command-and-control' management style that, we were told, nevertheless persists, particularly around performance management and especially in larger urban forces, where a more 'muscular' leadership style was said to be prevalent.

4   For reviews, including discussion of the emergence of organisational justice as a field of research in the 1980s, see Colquitt (2008) and Colquitt et al (2001).

5   However, Alison Liebling and her colleagues have provided a series of analyses of prison regimes that focus on organisational justice within prison management and procedural justice in dealings with prisoners, though without explicitly locating their work in either of these theoretical frameworks (see, for example, Liebling, 2004).

6   For findings from staff surveys in the UK, see Bradford and Quinton (2014) and Tankebe (2019). For a study of officers in Australia, see Roberts, Herrington and Hough (forthcoming).

7   The obvious exceptions being those who score low on ability to empathise but high on manipulative skills.

8   See Bottoms and Tankebe (2012) and Tankebe (2013, 2019).

9   See Wood, Tyler and Papachristos (2020).

10 There is, of course, an alternative and more critical account of professions as self-serving organisations designed to exclude competition and to maintain the benefits of their members.

11 These issues are considered in greater detail in Hough and Stanko (2018, 2019).

12 The What Works Centre for Crime Reduction, housed by the College of Policing (see: https://whatworks.college.police.uk/About/Pages/default. aspx).

13 The College of Policing produced the code of ethics (see: www.college. police.uk/What-we-do/Ethics/Ethics-home/Pages/Code-of-Ethics.aspx).

14 The College of Policing's Policing Education Qualification Framework specifies the requirements (see: www.college.police.uk/What-we-do/ Learning/Policing-Education-Qualifications-Framework/Pages/Policing-Education-Qualifications-Framework.aspx).

15 For a balanced statement of this perspective from a Police Federation briefing paper, see: www.polfed.org/Wilts/media/1580/policing-eductation-qualifications-framework-faqs.pdf

Chapter 6

1   This chapter draws on a previously unpublished paper co-authored by myself, Ben Bradford, Jon Jackson and Paul Quinton. I am grateful for their agreement to use this material.

2   The first extended discussion of these issues of which I am aware is that of MacCoun (2005).

3   For example, Article 1 of the Charter of Fundamental Rights of the European Union states that 'Human dignity is inviolable. It must be

respected and protected.' The charter will have no force in the UK when it leaves the European Union, of course.

4   One of the best-known examples of early social marketing is the poster first published in 1914, in which Lord Kitchener, Secretary of State for War, told potential volunteers for the British army: 'Your country needs you.'

5   The BIT is now independent of the Cabinet Office but part-owned by it (see: www.bi.team).

6   This definition of nudges is taken Thaler and Sunstein's (2008) book *Nudge: Improving Decisions about Health, Wealth and Happiness.*

7   See, eg, Daniel Kahneman's 2011 book, *Thinking Fast and Slow.*

8   This lack of clarity reflects the fact that policing in the UK is on a path towards increasing professionalisation, with uncertainty about the likely end point of this process. Some professions, such as healthcare, clearly expect practitioners to hold both competences and a set of ethical values. Others require competences with a much looser connection to ethical standards.

9   For evidence that religion can serve as a palliative to social conditions, see Jost et al (2014).

10   It should also be stressed that our knowledge of the Peelian principles is refracted through, and possibly distorted by, the accounts of mid-20th-century historians such as Reith (1956), whose primary sources are not readily available. For a discussion, see Lentz and Chaires (2007).

11   This is a version of the dilemma facing any reform-minded criminologist who sees connections between crime and social injustice.

Chapter 7

1   See: www.gmc-uk.org/ethical-guidance. There is no such reference to values in the Gas Safe Register (previously CORGI) that plumbers are required by law to sign up to (see: www.gassaferegister.co.uk/).

2   This was the title of a classic paper on police work by Cumming et al (1965) that documented the range and variety of police work. Similar studies appeared in the UK in the 1970s, charting the 'social work function' of the police (for example, Punch, 1979). The best-known television cop at this time was Constable George Dixon, later promoted to sergeant, in *Dixon of Dock Green*, a television series that ran from 1955 to 1976. Dixon embodied the ideal of the British bobby – dependable, resilient, empathetic and with what Kenneth Muir (1977) would call a 'tragic sense', that is, an appreciation of the human condition, accompanied by a well-developed moral perspective. For an analysis of the way in which the programme helped to create and sustain the myth of the British police, see Reiner (1994, 2008).

3   Robert Reiner (1978) dubbed these 'New Centurions', after the Joseph Wambaugh novel of this name. Also, for a discussion of the film character Dirty Harry, played by Clint Eastwood, see Klockars (1980). Raymond Chandler's private detective Philip Marlowe also shares these qualities.

4   See: www.college.police.uk/What-we-do/Ethics/Documents/Code_of_ Ethics.pdf

⁵ For a fuller discussion, see Hough and Sato (2014).

⁶ At the same time, definitions in law of what counts as unacceptable harm have been extended in some areas. Examples include hate crimes and coercive and sexually oppressive behaviour within relationships. For a discussion, see Jacobson and Hough (2018).

⁷ See, for example, Feinberg (1984), Miller (2010), Dworkin (1999) and Cane (2006).

⁸ See: http://psi329.cankaya.edu.tr/uploads/files/Devlin%2C%20The%20 Enforcement%20of%20Morals%20%281959%29%281%29.pdf

⁹ See Robinson and Darley (1997, 2004). Their starting point is that the evidence on the deterrent effects of punishment is too weak to provide a basis for decisions about appropriate punishments, and their conclusion is that shared public intuitions about the weight of punishment provides a firmer rationale, which will also bolster public judgements about judicial legitimacy.

¹⁰ However, one consequence of the COVID-19 pandemic may have been to restore a degree of confidence in scientific expertise, and dent the enthusiasm of 'anti-vaxxers'.

Postscript

¹ For the government's initial 'Action Plan', published on 3 March, see: www.gov.uk/government/publications/coronavirus-action-plan/ coronavirus-action-plan-a-guide-to-what-you-can-expect-across-the-uk

² The modelling, by Professor Neil Ferguson of Imperial College, has itself been subsequently challenged as being too pessimistic – though media coverage of the criticisms associates some of them with ideological opposition to the principle of lockdowns.

³ Figures taken on 29 May 2020 from the Johns Hopkins Coronavirus Resource Center (see: https://coronavirus.jhu.edu) and from the UK government's website for guidance on COVID-19 issues (see: www. gov.uk/guidance/coronavirus-covid-19-information-for-the-public). The 60,000 estimate of 'extra deaths' is drawn from monthly figures of excess deaths published by the Office of National Statistics. Figures for the first nine weeks of high prevalence of COVID-19 in March to May were not published in a specific report by ONS, but were widely reported in the press. EG www.ft.com/content/ 4a91a414-4937-4c54-aa78-6d231f4a4e43

⁴ See, for example, an interview by the director of the European Centre for Disease Prevention and Control, available at: www.theguardian.com/world/2020/may/20/ top-eu-doctor-europe-should-brace-itself-for-second-wave-of-coronavirus

⁵ SIs are a form of secondary legislation that typically fill in the detail of primary legislation when this sets out powers in only general terms. SIs are laid before Parliament and subject to only a light level of parliamentary scrutiny.

[6] See: www.legislation.gov.uk/uksi/2020/350/contents/made. Parallel statutory instruments set out similar regulations in Wales (see: www.legislation.gov.uk/wsi/2020/353/contents/made) and Scotland (see: www.legislation.gov.uk/ssi/2020/103/contents/made).

[7] See: www.legislation.gov.uk/uksi/2020/500/made

[8] The government guidance can be found at: www.gov.uk/government/publications/covid-19-stay-at-home-guidance/stay-at-home-guidance-for-households-with-possible-coronavirus-covid-19-infection

[9] See Fancourt et al (2020).

[10] The Nuffield-funded UCL survey shows a consistent difference in the ability to deal with the lockdown between young and economically precarious people, and their more affluent elders (see Fancourt et al, 2020).

[11] Statistics are from the National Police Chiefs Council (see: https://news.npcc.police.uk/resources/england-data-set).

[12] See: www.spectator.co.uk/article/former-supreme-court-justice-this-is-what-a-police-state-is-like-

[13] See: www.cps.gov.uk/legal-guidance/coronavirus-health-protection-coronavirus-restrictions-england-regulations-2020

[14] See: www.politico.eu/article/boris-johnson-risks-dragging-brits-out-of-coronavirus-lockdown-against-their-will/

[15] See: https://yougov.co.uk/topics/health/articles-reports/2020/05/11/brits-split-changes-coronavirus-lockdown-measures?utm_source=twitter&utm_medium=website_article&utm_campaign=snap_lockdown_loosening

[16] See: www.bbc.co.uk/news/uk-scotland-52177171

[17] See: www.bbc.co.uk/news/uk-politics-52553229

[18] See: https://www.durham.police.uk/news-and-events/Pages/News%20Articles/Durham-Constabulary-press-statement--.aspx

[19] See: www.bbc.co.uk/news/uk-politics-52782913

[20] See: https://reutersinstitute.politics.ox.ac.uk/trust-uk-government-and-news-media-covid-19-information-down-concerns-over-misinformation

References

Allen, R. and Hough, M. (2008) 'Does it matter? Reflections on the effectiveness of institutionalised public participation in the development of sentencing policy', in K. Gelb and A. Freiberg (eds) *Penal Populism: Sentencing Councils and Sentencing Policy*. Cullompton: Willan Publishing/Federation Press.

Ayres, I. and Braithwaite, J. (1992) *Responsive Regulation: Transcending the Deregulation Debate*. Oxford: Oxford University Press. Available at: http://johnbraithwaite.com/wp-content/uploads/2016/06/Responsive-Regulation-Transce.pdf

Beetham, D. (1991) *The Legitimation of Power*. London: Macmillan.

Bell, E. (2013) 'Normalising the exceptional: British colonial policing cultures come home', *Mémoire(s), identité(s), marginalité(s) dans le monde occidental contemporain*. Available at: https://doi.org/10.4000/mimmoc.1286

Bittner, E. (1970) *The Functions of the Police in Modern Society*. Chevy Chase, MD: National Institute of Mental Health.

Bittner, E. (1974) 'Florence Nightingale in pursuit of Willie Sutton: A theory of the police', in H. Jacobs (ed) *The Potential of Reform in Criminal Justice*. Beverly Hills, CA: Sage.

Blake, P., McAuliffe, K., Corbit, J., Callaghan, T.C., Barry, O., Bowie, A., Kleutsch, L., Kramer, K.L., Ross, E., Vongsachang, H., Wrangham, R. and Warneken, F. (2015) 'The ontogeny of fairness in seven societies', *Nature*, 528: 258–61. Available at: www.nature.com/articles/nature15703

Bottoms, A. (2002) 'Compliance and community penalties', in A. Bottoms, L. Gelsthorpe and S. Rex (eds) *Community Penalties: Change and Challenges*. Cullompton: Willan, pp 87–116.

Bottoms, A.E. and Tankebe, J. (2012) 'Beyond procedural justice: A dialogic approach to legitimacy in criminal justice', *Journal of Criminal Law and Criminology*, 102: 119–70.

Bowling, B. and Phillips, C. (2002) *Racism, Crime and Justice*. Harlow: Pearson Education.

Bradford, B. (2014) 'Policing and social identity: Procedural justice, inclusion, and cooperation between police and public', *Policing and Society*, 24(1): 22–43.

Bradford, B. (2020) 'Procedural justice – the impact of a theory', in C. Stott, B. Bradford, M. Radburn and L. Savigar-Shaw (eds) *Making an Impact on Policing and Crime*, Routledge Psychological Impacts Series, Abingdon: Routledge.

Bradford, B. and Jackson, J. (2018) 'Police legitimacy among immigrants in Europe: Institutional frames and group position', *European Journal of Criminology*, 15(5): 567–88.

Bradford, B. and Quinton, P. (2014) 'Self-legitimacy, police culture and support for democratic policing in an English Constabulary', *British Journal of Criminology*, 54(6): 1023–46.

Bradford, B., Murphy, K. and Jackson, J. (2014a) 'Officers as mirrors: Policing, procedural justice and the (re)production of social identity', *British Journal of Criminology*, 54(4): 527–50.

Bradford, B., Huq, A., Jackson, J. and Roberts, B. (2014b) 'What price fairness when security is at stake? Police legitimacy in South Africa', *Regulation and Governance*, 8(2): 246–68.

Bradford, B., Hohl, K., Jackson, J. and MacQueen, S. (2015) 'Obeying the rules of the road', *Journal of Contemporary Criminal Justice*, 31(2): 171–91.

Bradford, B., Sargeant, E., Murphy, T. and Jackson, J. (2017) 'A leap of faith? Trust in the police among migrants in England and Wales', *British Journal of Criminology*, 57(2): 381–401.

Braithwaite, J. (2017) 'Types of responsiveness', in P. Drahos (ed) *Regulatory Theory: Foundations and Applications*. Canberra: Australian National University Press. Available at: https://press-files.anu.edu.au/downloads/press/n2304/pdf/book.pdf

Braithwaite, V. (2017) 'Closing the gap between regulation and the community', in P. Drahos (ed) *Regulatory Theory: Foundations and Applications*. Canberra: Australian National University Press. Available at: https://press-files.anu.edu.au/downloads/press/n2304/pdf/book.pdf

Cane, P. (2006) 'Taking law seriously: Starting points of the Hart/Devlin debate', *The Journal of Ethics*, 10(1/2): 21–51.

Cartwright, N. and Hardie, J. (2012) *Evidence-Based Policy: A Practical Guide to Doing It Better*. Oxford: Oxford University Press.

College of Policing (2020) *Policing the Pandemic: The Act, the Regulations and Guidance*. London: College of Policing. www. college.police.uk/What-we-do/Support/Health-safety/ Documents/Policing_the_pandemic.pdf

Colquitt, J.A. (2008) 'Two decades of organisational justice: Findings, controversies and future directions', in C.L. Cooper and J. Barling (eds) *The Sage Handbook of Organizational Behavior, Volume 1: Micro Approaches*. Newbury Park, CA: Sage, pp 73–88.

Colquitt, J., Conlon, D., Wesson, M., Porter, C. and Ng, K. (2001) 'Justice at the millennium: A meta-analytic review of 25 years of organizational justice research', *Journal of Applied Psychology*, 86(3): 424–48. Available at: www.researchgate. net/publication/11920237_Justice_at_the_Millennium_A_ Meta-Analytic_Review_of_25_Years_of_Organizational_ Justice_Research

Coyle, A. (2009) *A Human Rights Approach to Prison Management: A Handbook for Prison Staff*. London: International Centre for Prison Studies. Available at: www.prisonstudies.org/sites/ default/files/resources/downloads/handbook_2nd_ed_eng_ 8.pdf

Cumming, E., Cumming, I. and Edell, L. (1965) 'The policeman and philosopher, guide and friend', *Social Problems*, 12(3): 276–86.

Drahos, P. (ed) (2017) *Regulatory Theory: Foundations and Applications*. Canberra: Australian National University Press. Available at: https://press-files.anu.edu.au/downloads/press/ n2304/pdf/book.pdf

Dworkin, G. (1999) 'Devlin was right: Law and the enforcement of morality', *William and Mary Law Review*, 40(3): 927–46.

Eisner, M. (2003) 'Long-term historical trends in violent crime', *Crime and Justice*, 30: 83–142. Available at: www.researchgate. net/profile/Manuel_Eisner/publication/279936907_ Long-Term_Historical_Trends_in_Violent_Crime/links/ 00b4952cdb00389a86000000/Long-Term-Historical-Trends-in-Violent-Crime.pdf

Eisner, M. (2014) 'From swords to words', *Crime and Justice*, 43: 65–134.

Elias, N. (1997 [1939]) *The Civilizing Process*. Oxford: Blackwell.

Enzmann, D., Kivivuori, J., Marshall, I.H., Steketee, M., Hough, M. and Killias, M. (2018) *A Global Perspective on Young People As Offenders and Victims. First Results from the ISRD3 Study*. New York, NY: Springer.

Fancourt, D., Bu, F., Mak, H.W. and Steptoe, A. (2020) *COVID-19 Social Study: Results Release 9*. York: Nuffield Foundation. Available at: https://mk0nuffieldfounpg9ee.kinstacdn.com/wp-content/uploads/2020/04/COVID-19-social-study-results-release-20-May-2020.pdf

Farrall, S. and Hay, C. (2014) *The Legacy of Thatcherism: Assessing and Exploring Thatcherite Social and Economic Policies*. Oxford: Oxford University Press.

Farrall, S., Jennings, W., Gray, E. and Hay, C. (2017) 'Thatcherism, crime and the legacy of the social and economic storms of the 1980s', *Howard Journal of Crime and Justice*, 56(2): 220–43.

Farren, D. and Hough, M. (2018a) 'Teenagers' perceptions of legitimacy and preparedness to break the law: The impact of migrant and ethnic minority status', in S. Roché and M. Hough (eds) *Minority Youth and Social Integration. The ISRD-3 Study in Europe and the US*. Cham: Springer International Publishing, pp 219–43.

Farren, D., Hough, M., Murray, K. and McVie, S. (2018b) 'Trust in the police and police legitimacy through the eyes of teenagers', in S. Roché and M. Hough (eds) *Minority Youth and Social Integration. The ISRD-3 Study in Europe and the US*. New York, NY: Springer, pp 167–92.

Fehr, E., Bernhard, H. and Rockenbach, B. (2008) 'Egalitarianism in young children', *Nature*, 454: 1079–83. Available at: https://doi.org/10.1038/nature07155

Feinberg, J. (1984) *Harm to Others*. Oxford: Oxford University Press.

Hales, G., May, T. Belur, J. and Hough, M. (2015) *Chief Officer Misconduct in Policing: An Exploratory Study*. London: College of Policing. Available at: https://whatworks.college.police.uk/Research/Documents/150317_Chief_officer_misconduct_FINAL_%20REPORT.pdf

Hales, J., Du Pont, S., Desroches, C. and Redgrave, H. (2020) *What Is Driving Serious Violence: Drugs*. London: Crest Advisory. Available at: www.crestadvisory.com/post/ understanding-what-is-driving-serious-violence-drugs

Harkin, D. (2015) 'Police legitimacy, ideology and qualitative methods: A critique of procedural justice theory', *Criminology and Criminal Justice*, 5: 594–612.

Hinsch, W. (2008) 'Legitimacy and justice', in J. Kuhnelt (ed) *Political Legitimation without Morality?* London: Springer.

Hinsch, W. (2010) 'Justice, legitimacy, and constitutional rights', *Critical Review of International Social and Political Philosophy*, 13(1): 39–54.

Home Affairs Select Committee (2018) 'Orgreave: Committee publishes letter to the Home Secretary on police files'. Available at: https://committees.parliament.uk/committee/83/ home-affairs-committee/news/100789/orgreave-committee-publishes-letter-to-the-home-secretary-on-police-files/

Hough, M. (2013) 'Procedural justice and professional policing in times of austerity', *Criminology and Criminal Justice*, 13(2): 181–97.

Hough, M. and Sato, M. (2014) 'D-5.1 report on compliance with the law: How normative and instrumental compliance interact', in S. Maffei and L. Markopoulou (eds) *FIDUCIA: New European Crimes and Trust-Based Policies. Volume 2.* Parma: University of Parma. Available at: www.fiduciaproject.eu/media/ publications/12/FiduciaV2_web.pdf

Hough, M. and Stanko, B. (2018) *Developing an Evidence Based Police Degree Holder Entry Programme: Final Report.* London: MOPAC. Available at: www.london.gov.uk/sites/ default/files/debpdhp_report_final.pdf

Hough, M. and Stanko, E.A. (2019) 'Designing degree-level courses for police recruits in England and Wales: Some issues and challenges', *Policing: A Journal of Policy and Practice*. Available at: https://academic.oup.com/policing/advance-article/doi/ 10.1093/police/pay096/5281217

Hough, M., Jackson, J. and Bradford, B. (2013) 'Trust in justice and the legitimacy of legal authorities: Topline findings from a European comparative study', in S. Body-Gendrot, M. Hough, R. Levy, K. Kerezsi and S. Snacken (eds) *European Handbook of Criminology*. London: Routledge.

Hough, M., May, T., Hales, G. and Belur, J. (2016) 'Misconduct by police leaders in England and Wales: An exploratory study', *Policing & Society*. Available at: http://dx.doi.org/10.1080/10439463.2016.1216989

Huq, A.Z., Tyler, T.R. and Schulhofer, S.J. (2011a) 'Mechanisms for eliciting cooperation in counterterrorism policing: Evidence from the United Kingdom', *Journal of Empirical Legal Studies*, 8(4): 728–61.

Huq, A.Z., Tyler, T.R. and Schulhofer, S.J. (2011b) 'Why does the public cooperate with law enforcement? The influence of the purposes and targets of policing', *Psychology, Public Policy, and Law*, 17(3): 419.

Huq, A.Z., Jackson, J. and Trinkner, R. (2017) 'Legitimating practices: Revisiting the predicates of police legitimacy', *British Journal of Criminology*, 57(5): 1101–22. Available at: https://doi.org/10.1093/bjc/azw037

Huxley, A. (1932) *Brave New World*. London: Chatto and Windus.

IPCC (Independent Police Complaints Commission) (2015) *Annex 1: IPCC Review of Matters Relating to the Policing of Events at Orgreave Coking Plant in 1984*. London: Independent Police Complaints Commission. Available at: www.statewatch.org/news/2015/jun/ippc-ogreave-review.pdf

Jackson, J. (2018) 'Norms, normativity and the legitimacy of legal authorities: International perspectives', *Annual Review of Law and Social Science*, 14: 145–165.

Jackson, J. and Bradford, B. (2019) 'Blurring the distinction between empirical and normative legitimacy? A methodological commentary on police legitimacy and citizen cooperation in China', *Asian Journal of Criminology*, 14: 265–89. Available at: https://doi.org/10.1007/s11417-019-09289-w

Jackson, J., Bradford, B., Hough, M., Kuha, J., Stares, S.R., Widdop, S., Fitzgerald, R., Yordanova, M. and Galev, T. (2011a) 'Developing European indicators of trust in justice', *European Journal of Criminology*, 8(4): 267–86.

Jackson, J., Hough, M., Bradford, B., Pooler, T., Hohl, K. and Kuha, J. (2011b) *Trust in Justice: Topline Results from Round 5 of the European Social Survey. ESS Topline Results Series Issue 1.* London: City University.

Jackson, J., Bradford, B., Hough, M., Myhill, A., Quinton, P. and Tyler, T. (2012) 'Why do people comply with the law? Legitimacy and the influence of legal institutions', *British Journal of Criminology*, 52(6): 1051–71.

Jackson, J., Asif, M., Bradford, B. and Zakar, M.Z. (2014) 'Corruption and police legitimacy in Lahore, Pakistan', *British Journal of Criminology*, 54: 1067–88.

Jackson, J., Hough, M., Bradford, B. and Kuha, J. (2015) 'Empirical legitimacy as two connected psychological states', in G. Mesko and J. Tankebe (eds) *Trust and Legitimacy in Criminal Justice: European Perspectives*, London: Springer, pp 137–60.

Jackson, J., Posch, K., Oliveira, T., Bradford, B., Mendes, S., Natal, A. and Zanetic, A. (2020) 'Fear and legitimacy in São Paulo, Brazil: Police–citizen relations in a high violence, high fear city'. Available at: https://osf.io/preprints/socarxiv/3awrz/

Jacobson, J. and Hough, M. (2018) 'Missed opportunities and new risks: penal policy in England and Wales in the past twenty-five years', *Political Quarterly*, 89(2): 177–86.

Johnson, B. (2019) 'Left wingers will howl. But it's time to make criminals afraid – not the public' *The Mail on Sunday*, 11 August.

Jost, J.T., Liviatan, I., Van der Toorn, J., Ledgerwood, A., Mandisodza, A. and Nosek, B.A. (2010) 'System justification: How do we know it's motivated?', in R. Bobocel, A.C. Kay, M.P. Zanna and J.M. Olson (eds) *The Psychology of Justice and Legitimacy: The Ontario Symposium* (vol 11). Hillsdale, NJ: Erlbaum, pp 173–203.

Jost, J.T., Hawkins, C.B., Nosek, B.A., Hennes, E.P., Stern, C., Gosling, S.D. and Graham, J. (2014) 'Belief in a just god (and a just society): A system justification perspective on religious ideology', *Journal of Theoretical and Philosophical Psychology*, 34: 56–81.

Kahneman, D. (2011) *Thinking, Fast and Slow*. Basingstoke: Macmillan.

Kerner Commission (1968) *Report of the National Advisory Commission on Civil Disorders*. Washington, DC: US Government Printing Office.

Klockars, C.B. (1980) 'The Dirty Harry problem', *Annals of the American Academy of Political and Social Science, Vol. 452, The Police and Violence*, November: 33–47. Available at: www.kyoolee.net/Dirty_Harry_Problem__the_-_Klockars.pdf

Lammy, D. (2017) *The Lammy Review: An Independent Review into the Treatment of, and Outcomes for, Black, Asian and Minority Ethnic Individuals in the Criminal Justice System*. London: Lammy. Available at: https://assets.publishing.service.gov.uk/government/uploads/system/uploads/attachment_data/file/643001/lammy-review-final-report.pdf

Lentz, S.A. and Chaires, R.H. (2007) 'The invention of Peel's principles: A study of policing "textbook" history', *Journal of Criminal Justice*, 35(1): 69–79. Available at: www.sciencedirect.com/science/article/pii/S0047235206001449

Liebling, A. (2004) *Prisons and Their Moral Performance: A Study of Values, Quality, and Prison Life*. Oxford: Oxford University Press.

Loader, I. and Mulcahy, A. (2003) *Policing and the Condition of England: Memory, Politics and Culture*. Oxford: Oxford University Press.

Loader, I. and Sparks, R. (2013) 'Unfinished business: Legitimacy, crime control and democratic politics', in J. Tankebe and A. Liebling (eds) *Legitimacy and Criminal Justice: An International Exploration*. Oxford: Oxford University Press.

Lukes, S. (2005) *Power: A Radical View*. London: Palgrave Macmillan.

MacCoun, R.J. (2005) 'Voice, control and belonging: The double-edged sword of procedural fairness', *Annual Review of Law and Social Science*, 1: 419–43. Available at: www.annualreviews.org/doi/abs/10.1146/annurev.lawsocsci.1.041604.115958

Macpherson, W. (1999) *The Stephen Lawrence Inquiry: Report of an Inquiry by Sir William Macpherson. Cm 4262-I*. London: HMSO. Available at: https://assets.publishing.service.gov.uk/government/uploads/system/uploads/attachment_data/file/277111/4262.pdf

MacQueen, S. and Bradford, B. (2015) 'Enhancing public trust and police legitimacy during road traffic encounters: Results from a randomized controlled trial in Scotland', *Journal of Experimental Criminology*, 11(3): 419–43.

May, T., Gyateng, T. and Hough, M. (2010) *Differential Treatment in the Youth Justice System*. London: Equalities and Human Rights Commission.

Mazerolle, L., Antrobus, E., Bennett, S. and Tyler, T. (2013) 'Shaping citizen perceptions of police legitimacy: A randomised field trial of procedural justice', *Criminology*, 51(1): 33–63.

McBarnet, D. (1981) *Conviction: The Law, the State and the Construction of Justice*. Basingstoke: Palgrave Macmillan.

Meares, T.L. (2013) 'The good cop: Knowing the difference between lawful or effective policing and rightful policing – and why it matters', *William and Mary Law Review*, 54: 1865–86.

Meares, T.L., Tyler, T. and Gardener, J. (2015) 'Lawful or fair? How cops and laypeople view good policing', *The Journal of Criminal Law and Criminology*, 105(2): 297–344.

Messner, S.F. (2015) 'When West meets East: Generalizing theory and expanding the conceptual toolkit of criminology', *Asian Journal of Criminology*, 10(2): 117–29. Available at: www.ncbi.nlm.nih.gov/pubmed/27087864

Messner, S. and Rosenfeld, R. (2001) 'An institutional-anomie theory of crime', in R. Paternoster and R. Bachman (eds) *Explaining Criminals and Crime*. Los Angeles, CA: Roxbury.

Messner, S. and Rosenfeld, R. (2010) 'Institutional-anomie theory: A macro-sociological explanation of crime', in A.J.L. Krohn and G.P. Hall (eds) *Handbook on Crime and Deviance*. New York, NY: Springer Science – Business Media.

Miller, W. (2010) 'Conservatism and the Devlin–Hart debate', *International Journal of Politics and Good Governance*, 1(3): 1–20.

Mols, F., Haslam, S.A., Jetten, J. and Steffens, N.K. (2015) 'Why a nudge is not enough: A social identity critique of governance by stealth', *European Journal of Political Research*, 54: 81–98.

Muir, K.C. (1977) *Police: Streetcorner Politicians*. Chicago, IL: University of Chicago Press. Available at: https://www.amazon.com/Police-Streetcorner-William-Ker-Muir/dp/0226546330

Murphy, K. (2017) 'Procedural justice and its role in promoting voluntary compliance', in P. Drahos (ed) *Regulatory Theory: Foundations and Applications*. Canberra: Australian National University Press. Available at: https://press-files.anu.edu.au/downloads/press/n2304/pdf/book.pdf

Murray, K., McVie, S., Farren, D., Herlitz, L., Hough, M. and Norris, P. (2020) 'Procedural justice, compliance with the law and police stop-and-search: A study of young people in England and Scotland', *Policing and Society*, DOI: 10.1080/10439463.2020.1711756.

Nagin, D.S. and Telep, C.W. (2017) 'Procedural justice and legal compliance', *Annual Review of Law and Social Science*, 13(3): 5–28.

Newman, K. (1985) *The Metropolitan Police: The Principles of Policing and Guidance for Professional Behaviour*. London: Metropolitan Police Service.

Norrie, A. (2001) *Crime, Reason and History*. London: Butterworths.

Nye, J. (1990) *Bound to Lead: The Changing Nature of American Power*. London: Basic Books.

Oliveira, T.R., Jackson, J., Murphy, K. and Bradford, B. (forthcoming) 'Are trustworthiness and legitimacy "hard to win and easy to lose"? A longitudinal test of the asymmetry thesis of police–citizen contact'. Available at: https://osf.io/preprints/socarxiv/adhbm/

Orwell, G. (1949) *Nineteen Eighty-Four: A Novel*. London: Secker and Warburg.

Papachristos, A.V., Meares, T.L. and Fagan, J. (2012) 'Why do criminals obey the law? The influence of legitimacy and social networks on active gun offenders', *The Journal of Criminal Law and Criminology*, 102(2): 397–440.

Patten Report (1999) *A New Beginning: Policing in Northern Ireland*. Belfast: Independent Commission on Policing in Northern Ireland. Available at: https://cain.ulster.ac.uk/issues/police/patten/patten99.pdf

Phillips, C. (2019) 'The trouble with culture: A speculative account of the role of Gypsy/Traveller cultures in "doorstep fraud"', *Theoretical Criminology*, 23(3): 333–54. Available at: https://doi.org/10.1177/1362480617733725

Phillips, C. and Bowling, B. (2017) 'Ethnicities, racism, crime and criminal justice', in A. Liebling, S. Maruna and L. McAra (eds) *Oxford Handbook of Criminology* (6th edn). Oxford: Oxford University Press.

Pinker, S. (2011) *The Better Angels of Our Nature: Why Violence Has Declined.* London: Viking.

Pinker, S. (2018) *Enlightenment Now: The Case for Reason, Science, Humanism and Progress.* London: Allen Lane.

Posch, K., Jackson, J., Bradford, B. and MacQueen, S. (2020) ' "Truly free consent"? Clarifying the nature of police legitimacy using causal mediation analysis', *Journal of Experimental Criminology.* Available at: https://doi.org/10.1007/s11292-020-09426-x

President's Task Force (2015) *Final Report of the President's Task Force on 21st Century Policing.* Washington, DC: Office of Community Oriented Policing Services. Available at: https://cops.usdoj.gov/pdf/taskforce/taskforce_finalreport.pdf

Punch, M. (1979) 'The secret social service', in S. Holdaway (ed) *The British Police.* London: Edward Arnold.

Quattlebaum, Q., Meares, T. and Tyler, T. (2018) *Principles of Procedurally Just Policing.* Yale: Yale Law School. Available at: https://law.yale.edu/sites/default/files/area/center/justice/principles_of_procedurally_just_policing_report.pdf

Radburn, M. and Stott, C. (2019) 'The social psychological processes of "procedural justice": Concepts, critiques and opportunities', *Criminology and Criminal Justice,* 19(4): 421–38.

Ramsay, P. (2006) 'The responsible subject as citizen: Criminal law, democracy and the welfare state', *Modern Law Review,* 69(1): 29–58.

Reiner, R. (1978) *The Blue Coated Worker.* Cambridge: Cambridge University Press.

Reiner, R. (1994) 'The dialectics of Dixon: The changing image of the TV cop', in M. Stephens and S. Becker (eds) *Police Force, Police Service.* London: Macmillan.

Reiner, R. (2000) *The Politics of the Police* (3rd edn). Oxford: Oxford University Press.

Reiner, R. (2008) 'Policing and the media' in T. Newburn (ed) *Handbook of Policing* (2nd edn). Cullompton: Willan.

Reiner, R. (2010) *The Politics of the Police* (4th edn). Oxford: Oxford University Press.

Reiner, R. (2016) 'Is police culture cultural?', *Policing: A Journal of Policy and Practice*, 11(3): 236–41.

Reith, C. (1956) *A New Study of Police History*. London: Oliver and Boyd.

Roberts, J.V., Stalans, L.S., Indermaur, D. and Hough, M. (2003) *Penal Populism and Public Opinion. Findings from Five Countries.* New York, NY: Oxford University Press.

Roberts, K., Herrington, V. and Hough, M. (forthcoming) 'Organisational justice and officer wellbeing: What next for police leaders?'

Robinson, P.H. and Darley, J.M. (1997) 'The utility of desert', *Northwestern University Law Review*, 91: 453–99.

Robinson, P.H. and Darley, J.M. (2004) 'Does criminal law deter? A behavioural science investigation', *Oxford Journal of Legal Studies*, 24: 173–205.

Roché, S. and Hough, M. (2018) *Minority Youth and Social Integration: The ISRD-3 Study in Europe and the US.* New York: Springer.

Saunders, P. (2010) *Beware False Prophets: Equality, the Good Society and The Spirit Level.* London: Policy Exchange.

Scarman, Lord (1981) *The Brixton Disorders: Report of an Inquiry by the Rt. Hon. Lord Scarman OBE.* London: HMSO.

Schulhofer, S.J., Tyler, T.R. and Huq, A.Z. (2011) 'American policing at a crossroads: Unsustainable policies and the procedural justice alternative', *The Journal of Criminal Law and Criminology*, 101(2): 335–74.

Sherman, L.W. (1993) 'Defiance, deterrence and irrelevance: A theory of the criminal sanction', *Journal of Research in Crime and Delinquency*, 30(4): 445–73.

Skogan, W. (2006) 'Asymmetry in the impact of encounters with the police', *Policing and Society*, 16(2): 99–126.

Skogan, W. and Frydl, K. (2004) *Fairness and Effectiveness in Policing: The Evidence.* Washington, DC: The National Academies Press. Available at: www.nap.edu/read/10419/chapter/1

Skogan, W., Van Craen, M. and Hennessy, C. (2015) 'Training police for procedural justice', *Journal of Experimental Criminology*, 11(3): 319–34.

Skolnick, J. (1966) *Justice Without Trial*. New York, NY: Wiley.

Sun, I.Y., Li, L., Wu, Y. and Hu, R. (2018) 'Police legitimacy and citizen cooperation in China: Testing an alternative model', *Asian Journal of Criminology*, 13(4): 275–91.

Sunshine, J. and Tyler, T.R. (2003) 'The role of procedural justice and legitimacy in shaping public support for policing', *Law and Society Review*, 37(3): 513–48.

Tajfel, H. and Turner, J.C. (1979) 'An integrative theory of intergroup conflict', in W.G. Austin and S. Worchel (eds) *The Social Psychology of Intergroup Relations*. Monterey: Brooks/Cole, pp 33–47.

Tajfel, H. and Turner, J.C. (1986) 'The social identity theory of intergroup behaviour', in S. Worchel and W.G. Austin (eds) *Psychology of Intergroup Relations*. Chicago, IL: Nelson-Hall, pp 7–24.

Tankebe, J. (2013) 'Viewing things differently: The dimensions of public perceptions of police legitimacy', *Criminology*, 51(1): 103–35.

Tankebe, J. (2019) 'In their own eyes: An empirical examination of police self-legitimacy', *International Journal of Comparative and Applied Criminal Justice*, 43(2): 99–116. Available at: https://doi.org/10.1080/01924036.2018.1487870

Thaler, R.H. and Sunstein, C.R. (2008) *Nudge: Improving Decisions about Health, Wealth and Happiness*. Boston, MA: Yale University Press.

The Guardian (2017) 'The Scandal of Orgreave', 18 May. Available at: www.theguardian.com/politics/2017/may/18/scandal-of-orgreave-miners-strike-hillsborough-theresa-may

Thibaut, J.W. and Walker, L. (1975) *Procedural Justice: A Psychological Analysis*. Hillsdale, NJ: Erlbaum.

Tsushima, M. and Hamai, K. (2015) 'Public cooperation with the police in Japan', *Journal of Contemporary Criminal Justice*, 31(2): 212–28.

Tyler, T.R. (2003) 'Procedural justice, legitimacy, and the effective rule of law', in M. Tonry (ed) *Crime and Justice: A Review of Research, 30*. Chicago, IL: University of Chicago Press, pp 431–505.

Tyler, T.R. (2006) *Why People Obey the Law*. Princeton, NJ: Princeton University Press.

Tyler, T.R. (2011a) *Why People Cooperate: The Role of Social Motivations*. Princeton, NJ: Princeton University Press.

Tyler, T.R. (2011b) 'Trust and legitimacy: Policing in the USA and Europe', *European Journal of Criminology*, 8(4): 254–66.

Tyler, T.R. and Fagan, J. (2008) 'Why do people cooperate with the police?', *Ohio State Journal of Criminal Law*, 6: 231–75.

Tyler, T.R. and Jackson, J. (2014) 'Popular legitimacy and the exercise of legal authority: Motivating compliance, cooperation, and engagement', *Psychology, Public Policy, and Law*, 20(1): 78–95.

Tyler, T.R. and Trinkner, R. (2017) *Why Children Follow Rules: Legal Socialization and the Development of Legitimacy*. Oxford: Oxford University Press.

Tyler, T.R., Schulhofer, S.J. and Huq, A.Z. (2010) 'Legitimacy and deterrence effects in counter-terrorism policing: A study of Muslim Americans', *Law and Society Review*, 44: 365–401.

Tyler, T.R., Jackson, J. and Mentovich, A. (2015) 'The consequences of being an object of suspicion: Potential pitfalls of proactive police contact', *Journal of Empirical Legal Studies*, 12(4): 602–36.

Van Dijk, J. (2013) 'It is not just the economy: towards an alternative explanation of post-World War II crime trends in the Western world', in S. Body-Gendrot, M. Hough, R. Levy, K. Kerezsi and S. Snacken (eds) *European Handbook of Criminology*. London: Routledge.

Weitzer, R. and Tuch, S.A. (2006) *Race and Policing in America: Conflict and Reform*. Cambridge: Cambridge University Press.

Wheller, L., Quinton, P., Fildes, A. and Mills, A. (2013) *The Greater Manchester Police Procedural Justice Training Experiment: The Impact of Communication Skills Training on Officers and Victims of Crime.* London: College of Policing. Available at: www.researchgate.net/publication/283348401_The_Greater_Manchester_Police_Procedural_Justice_Experiment_The_Impact_of_Communication_Skills_Training_on_Officers_and_Victims_of_Crime

Wikström, P.O., Oberwittler, D., Treiber, K. and Hardie, B. (2012) *Breaking Rules: The Social and Situational Dynamics of Young People's Urban Crime.* Oxford: Oxford University Press.

Wilkinson, R. and Pickett, K. (2009) *The Spirit Level: Why More Equal Societies Almost Always Do Better.* London: Allen Lane.

Wood, G., Tyler, T. and Papachristos, A. (2020) 'Procedural justice training reduces police misconduct and use of force', *Proceedings of the National Academy of Science of the United States.* Available at: www.pnas.org/cgi/doi/10.1073/pnas.1920671117

Index

Note: References to figures are in *italics* and to tables are in **bold**; references to endnotes are the page number followed by the note number (231n3).